First published in Great Britain in 1998 by
POETRY NOW
1-2 Wainman Road, Woodston,
Peterborough, PE2 7BU
Telephone (01733) 230746
Fax (01733) 230751

All Rights Reserved

Copyright Contributors 1998

SB ISBN 1 86188 768 X

FOREWORD

The tragic death of Diana, Princess of Wales devastated millions of people around the world. The images of thousands of mourners laying flowers at Kensington, St James' and Buckingham Palace are not easily forgotten.

The eerie silence that followed Diana's coffin through the streets of London and the harrowed faces of her two young sons, Princes William and Harry.

Elton John singing 'Candle In The Wind' is a memory that will not be forgotten and the emotion of Diana's favourite hymn 'I Pray To Thee My Country', will stay with many people for years to come.

Were the paparazzi to blame, was the chauffeur, Henri Paul drunk, was there another car involved? The answers to these questions are still being sought, but will anyone ever know the truth?

This anthology covers every aspect of Diana's death, with some truly inspiring and emotion charged poetry. The poets included have captured the thoughts and feelings of everyday people that will make this book an everlasting tribute to the life of: Diana, Princess of Wales.

CONTENTS

A Fond Farewell	Paul Secrett	1
Golden Days	Nigel David Evans	2
The Queen Of Hearts	Shirley Thompson	2
To HRH The Princess Of Wales	Lucy Carrington	3
The Rose Princess	Donna Joanne Kinsey	4
Diana, More Than A Princess	Neil Fisher	5
For Eternity	Richard Beeson	6
And The World Cried Too	Caroline Hartley	8
A Flower Lost Forever	David Whitney	9
Diana A Princess	Ray Jacks	10
In Memory Of Diana, The Princess Of Wales	Diane Godbold	11
Queen Of Hearts	Marie Evans	12
Diana	Tina Elener	12
All We Had	Linda Dickerson	13
Diana	Paul Birkitt	14
Untitled	Siân Kelly-Scott	15
Princess Diana	Pamela Eckhardt	16
A Tribute To Diana, Princess Of Wales	Angie J Gibbs	16
Diana, Princess Of Wales	Marian Curtis Jones	17
Farewell Princess Of Wales	Raymond Baggaley	18
Lady Sunshine	Valerie Marshall	19
Diana	Frank Henry	20
Princess Diana	Ann Burton	21
A Tribute To Diana	A W Harvey	21
May Flowers Grow	Mr & Mrs L Smith	22
Tribute To Diana	Hannah Birch	22
To The People's Princess	Anita Farrington	23

Forever In Our Thoughts	Helen Nelson	24
Princess Diana	Stephanie Bones	24
For The Love Of Diana	Vivienne M Wright	25
A Burning Candle	Jyoti Patel	26
Princess Of Smiles And Tears	P J Knightly	26
Diana	Jean	27
Just A Short Time	Judith Stevens	28
Farewell To A Princess	Jean McDonnell	29
Diana, Always	Caroline Amess	30
A 'Legend' In Her Lifetime	Dilys Parry	32
August 31st 1997	Nicky Handley	33
Diana	Debbie Allen	34
Together Forever	Allison Jones	34
Princess Of The People	Fred Tighe	35
A Tribute To Diana, Princess Of Wales	Rosaleen and Family	36
Diana - The People's Princess	Anne Adams	37
Diana - England's Rose	Jamie Redding	38
The Passing Of A Princess	Gary Long	39
Diana, Princess Of Wales 1961-1997	Christine Helen Cruse	40
Queen Of Hearts	Maria Smith	41
Princess Diana	Samantha Malster	42
Diana Queen Of Hearts	Sue Hamilton	43
Diana	Alan Graham	44
Hug	J Robson	45
Dear Diana	J Pearson	46
Diana	Sheila E McMillan	46
A Friend Of Friends	S J Davidson	47
Diana	Dinah Matthew	48
Our Princess	Margaret Phillips	49

Diana	Dennis Turner	50
A Moment To Live	Jessica Wright	50
Princess In The Sky	Vicky Dillingham	51
The People's Princess	M Craven	52
Angel	Ian Fowler	53
Lady Di	George Livingston Shand	54
A Tribute To The Late Diana, Princess Of Wales 1961-1997	Evelyn A Evans	55
Compassion Lost	John Bryan	56
Diana, Our Princess Of Wales	Sandra Sharp	56
To Diana	Iris McFarland	57
Diana - Queen Of Hearts	Josephine Giles	58
Diana	Marie O'Kane	60
Tribute To Diana	Richard Wolfendale	61
We Came From Miles Around	Philip Isle	62
Diana - The Legend	Christopher Downs	63
Diana	Simone Ryder	64
A Dark September Day	Ken Lowe	64
Our English Rose	Fiona Gilpin	65
Diana	Amanda-Lea Manning	66
In Memory Of Diana, Princess Of Wales	Lorraine Day	67
Diana, Princess Of Wales	Edna Hunt	68
God Lent Us An Angel	Susan May Downs	69
Final Journey Of A Princess	Bruno D'Itri	70
Princess	Lindsey Newrick	71
We Are Numb	Eileen M Lodge	72
To Princess Diana	Noel Egbert Williamson	72
A Princess - And A Mother	Pamela Evans	73
The People's Princess	Janette Campbell	74
Diana - Princess Of Wales	Gwyneth Cleworth	75

A Fond Farewell To Our Queen Of Hearts	Matt Valentine	76
A Princess, An Angel, A Friend	S Kirkley	77
Peace, Love And Diana	Nikki George	78
A Tribute To A Princess	Jayne M Lysyj	79
A Poet's Homage To Princess Diana	Tom Bull	80
Vocation	Glenna Towler	81
Princess Diana	Gwen Smith	82
Fond Memories Of Diana, Princess Of Wales (1961 -1997)	Brian Harris	83
Our Eternal - The Princess Diana	Olivia Lambeth	84
To Diana	Samantha Jayne Eley	85
Compassion	Beryl Cosgrave	86
A Prayer For A Princess	Maureen Owen	88
In Memory . . .	Graham Wickens	89
Poetic Tribute To Diana	A K Swann	89
Diana: A Requiem	Alan Pow	90
Our Princess Diana	Lillian Johnson	91
Glittering Star	Vivienne Doncaster	92
A Young Man's Princess	Gordon S Allen	92
Diana	Patricia Finney	93
For A Princess	Keith Barnard	94
O' Beloved Diana	Samia Chacko	94
Poem For Remembrance To Diana, Princess Of Wales	Janet Robinson	95
Diana	Arch Lang	96
Memories	Janet Brown	96
Diana The Lady We Love	Edna Adams	97

The Bruise-Laden Sky	J M Smith	98
Portrait Of Diana	Francis Paul Farnworth	98
Life Of A Princess	Moira M Michie	99
Dear Lord Up Above	S Bale	100
Gentle Diana	Patricia Tilling	100
Sunday 7th September 1997 'Afternoon'	Marlene Sarah Jones	101
The Princess Of The Lake	Rena Soloman	102
Parting Song For Diana	Elizabeth Ruskin	103
Eternal Love	Maureen J Archibold	104
In Memory Of Princess Diana	Kirsty Davies	105
Diana Princess Of Wales	Jean Tennent Mitchell	106
A Queen Of Hearts	Bell Ferris	107
The Fairy-Tale Princess	Rachael Taylor	108
My Tribute For Diana Is . . .	Victoria Hogan	109
Diana's Lullaby	Margaret Wendt	110
Diana Princess Of Wales	Lisa Wyatt	110
Eulogy To A Princess	Julia Eva Yeardye	111
A Tribute To Princess Diana	Gladys Davenport	112
Only A Minute	Elizabeth Mitchell	112
The Smile Of Love	Joan Smith	113
Diana Princess Of Love Remembered	Linda Coleman	114
Chronicle Of Memories	Jacki McEneaney	115
Simply Diana	Matthew J Prescott	116
Diana	Don Jeffery	117
A Star Shines Brightly	Doris Dobbins	117
Our Princess	P M Wardle	118
On Your Island Of Dreams	Jackie Goldsworthy	118
Diana	Betty Taylor	119
Many Years Of Love	Susan W Robinson	120

Diana - (Voice Of The World)	W G Royce	120
Rose In Paris	Gillian Ackers	121
Diana Sweet Princess	Darren Hennessy & Family	121
September Sadness	G Tominey	122
A Tribute To Diana	Gilbert Harford	122
A Tribute To Diana Princess Of Wales	Catherine Mary Smerdon	123
Diana	Pauline Christina Knight	123
Sleep Now, Sleep	Nicholas William Jones	124
A Sea Of Tears Out Of Sadness	B Fletcher	125
Lady Of The Lake	Janna Eliot	126
APicture Of Tragedy	Sylvia M Coulson	127
BBC1 London, September 6th 1997	John Matthews	128
Litany Of Diana	Mary Seddon	129
Beloved Diana	Lynne Stuart	130
The Silent Scents Of Remembrance	Barbara Keeling	131
Funeral Of Diana, Princess Of Wales	John Ernest Day	132
Diana Princess - Super Star	June White	133
The Blossoming Of Diana The White Rose	Pauline Morris	134
Memories Of A Beautiful Princess	Lisa Frost	135
Rest A While	Jacqueline Gilbert	136
Diana	Stella J Jefferies	137
To Diana	D Ridings	138
Diana Princess Of Wales	Ronald Finnighan	138
In Memory Of Diana, Princess Of Wales	Barbara I Grove	139

Farewell To Diana	Lindy Ess	139
Diana	Garrett John	140
Happiness	Mark McFall	140
To Diana	Peggy Adams	141
Lady Di	Lisa Hobden	142
She Deserved Respect And She Got It	Esther Austin	144
Diana	Pauline Haggett	145
Silence	Jennifer Packham	146
Diana	Kay Rainsley	147
Untitled	Richard Irvine	147
Princess Of Smiles	Margaret J H Goudie	148
Without You	Kate Susan Douglas	148
The Melody Lingers	Tamar Segal	149
Sombre Days	T A Peachey	150
Lament	Cynthia Beaumont	150
Tribute To Diana	B S Hansen	151
Tribute To Diana	Mick Philpot	151
Nos Star	Richard Beck	152
Princess Diana	Pamela Jewell	153
An Epitaph To A Real Lady	Sue Jackett	154
Earth's Rainbow Of Love	J S Mitchell	155
Dreams Of Light	Mel Leggett	156
Queen Of Hearts	Denise Margaret Hargrave	156
Diana The World's Princess	Ann Best	157
A Tribute	Samantha	158

A Fond Farewell

The nation has gathered,
Upon this sad day,
To say goodbye to a friend.
Like seeds we are scattered,
As each in our own way
But we are loyal right up to the end.

The memories we share,
Of those happy days,
We'll have 'til the end of time.
Those moments so rare,
And your special ways,
Keep coming back into mind.

Princess Diana with you,
Our hearts will remain,
As we say a tearful goodbye,
With feeling so true,
We just wish to say,
That we love you with so much pride.

So it's just left to say,
Just how sorry we feel,
As we bid you a fond farewell.
But maybe someday,
With feeling so real,
We'll remember how for you we all felt.

Paul Secrett

Golden Days

It's a splendid day in early spring,
I can hear the cuckoos and the linnets sing,
Overcome by apple blossom and bright sunshine,
Machiko and I descend the long incline.
Princess Diana has come to open a home,
And London Road is jam packed full with
                                             a throng.
We wait for the four car motorcade,
And Diana cheerfully smiles and waves,
Later, resplendent with hair so gold,
Each waiting hand she clasps and holds.
Such days are in the past now, and in the
                                            past remain,
Will such golden days for England ever
                                             come again?

Nigel David Evans

The Queen Of Hearts

How will we remember you?
We will remember, in a quiet moment in time.
The people's princess, loved and adored,
Taken from us, suddenly, a tragedy, a crime.

How will we remember you?
In our hearts, you will remain.
You cared, for all the little children,
Compassion for others, in suffering, in pain.

How will we remember you?
Shock and horror, at your tragic loss.
Our ambassador, for human rights,
We weigh up, the price, the cost.

How will we remember you?
For your beauty, world famous, renowned.
Charitable work, carried out, with a joke, a smile,
Through the years, you became, the jewel
                              in the crown.

Shirley Thompson

To HRH The Princess Of Wales

Always you awakened the world
to your regal charm and grace.
Like gems in bright light
you would sparkle and delight,
to captivate each soul and heart.
But your outer and inner beauty
combined made you stand out
as the unique jewel in the crown.
True, you were a shining example for
others how to behave.
So regal you were in every way,
how you walked, talked and smiled.
HRH was all over you stamped.
Once you were destined to become
the future Queen of the UK.
Now as such, in the nation's hearts
and minds, forever you will stay.

Lucy Carrington

The Rose Princess

*As shadows of grey shrouds over the Vale,
the heavy silver clouds gently float,
and sparkled rain falls for every crystal tear.*

*The empty sky, not a bird free in flight,
swaying trees whisper silently in the distance,
the whimpering sighs of the gasping world.*

*The air is crisp and clean, so sharp,
a life so precious, so lonely,
burning time can never take away the pain.*

*Winter chills are blowing near,
as every wave on the ocean waves,
soft snow will soon fall,
for our beautiful rose princess.*

*Endless questions are often unanswered,
as we gather our spirits together.*

*We celebrate one so filled with love,
for all the land can never forget,
the beautiful rose princess.*

*Strong and spirited,
loving and giving,
capturing and melting hearts.*

*But now we stand - one body,
one nation - forever.*

*Gone but never forgotten,
to our beautiful rose princess.*

Donna Joanne Kinsey

Diana, More Than A Princess

A queen that never was,
You will forever be,
Within our hearts,
As a queen should be.

At one with the people,
Everyone united in their grief,
The hands of friendship,
Shared in spontaneous applause.

Without pomp and ceremony galore,
Beauty to behold,
As unique as a flower,
Reigning as nature intended.

Silence in expression,
Disbelief in the facts,
As accident too common to know,
Awake to the mercy of fate.

Tears may flow from guilt or sorrow,
Ignorance excused if unborn,
Too many if onlys,
A future lost in memories.

Sorry for doubting your sincerity,
Humble to your actions unknown,
Let me grieve alone,
And pray for your accession into Heaven.

Neil Fisher

For Eternity

*I never met our Princess although,
strangely, somehow
Since her death 'tis almost like I've come to
know her now;
In the last few days from seeing her on the TV,
There were many things she did quite
unobtrusively,
Things that weren't reported at the time when
they were done,
Like sharing with the people her sense of
joy and fun,
Ordinary people at work, and in their homes too,
For them, if the need arose, doing what
she could do,
Giving to those who had lost it, for the
future, hope,
Helping them see, after all, that with life
they COULD cope;
Cheering up the elderly, the homeless
and the sad,
All despite the personal problems she also had;
To raise funds for charity she gladly lent
her weight,
Happily encouraging all those less fortunate;
Dealing with the landmines' scourge,
she made us all aware
Of the lives these fearful weapons, if not banned,
lay bare,
Although her humanity in EVERYTHING she did,
Beneath royal protocol would simply not be hid;
Stripped of being HRH, no scrap of diff'rence
made,
In fact helped increase for her the people's*

accolade;
Showing she was vulnerable, just like you and I,
Only served to heighten our feelings for Lady Di;
A Princess she may have been, yet one
of us no less,
Having to deal with life's problems,
ups and downs, and stress;
However, for living it was clear she had a thirst,
Likewise, as a loving mother, her two boys
came first;
But, out of the blue, then came that dreadful
August day
When, to be with Him, The Lord spirited
her away;
Who though could have known the grief and
sadness left behind?
Who, just the right words to express
their feelings, could find?
Why was it Diana had been given such a cup?
Surely it was a bad dream from which we'd
soon wake up;
Yet we had to face the truth, our Queen of Hearts
had gone,
Whilst, down her path, we must do our best to
follow on,
Giving of ourselves like Christ who, all those
years ago,
On a cross gave Self for us, that in Him we
might grow;
And, though we see darkly now, His risen llght
will guide,
Helping us to know that, even now, He's at
our side

> 'Til, when in His Father's house, our mansion
> is prepared,
> And love, in all it's fullness, for eternity
> is shared.

Richard Beeson

And The World Cried Too

August thirty-first nineteen ninety-seven,
Was a tragic day for Britain,
When our Princess was taken to heaven,
Such a sad loss,
To those she loved and knew,
Such a sad loss,
To those like me and you.
She touched the world with magic,
Made problems lighter with her smile,
She gave love to everyone,
That stretched from mile to mile,
Nobody can express,
All the inner pain we feel,
It's an enormous emotion,
That we can't seem to reveal,
But it wasn't just tears from Britain,
From the flowers and gifts we knew,
That the young and the old and
                    the rich and the poor,
And the whole world cried too.

Caroline Hartley

A Flower Lost Forever
(Inspired by the untimely death of the Princess of Wales, Diana)

A flower lost forever
But the perfume lingers on
A life as sweet as music
So you'll not forget the song
A world lost in its hunger
For the greedy ones to feed
Forgetting love's humanity
The wanting and the need
A touch of someone's caring
Wearing heart upon her sleeve
So short a stay of kindness
Why in God's name should you leave?
Your work, a worldwide effort
Sowing seeds of hope and love
Too good to live in this life
You were wanted up above
But though your smile's a memory
It's a smile that will not die
It was blessed with every angel's kiss
And though we're bound to cry
We won't forget you princess
You were special to us all
And though we cried the loudest
You responded to God's call
So dear flower lost forever
Let your perfume linger on
You'll be with us now forever
So you haven't really gone.

David Whitney

Diana A Princess

Golden hair, sad eyes, gorgeous smile, coy look
Features of a Princess from a story book
Alas this is not fiction
It is a real Lady, with a love addiction.

Into railway sidings, late at night would go
For loving secret meetings, with her Royal beau
From these secret meetings, romance grew
and grew
Until Her Royal Prince said, 'I really do love you.'

A ring upon her finger, with the world she
shared her joy
She really thought at this time, she had
got her boy
A wedding later followed, a day of regal grace
That look of loving feelings showed upon her face

Out of that Cathedral, stepped our Lady Di
She had now become a Princess, looking
oh so shy
It had always been a dream, a Prince for her
to marry
As time went by along came sons, William
and Harry.

A veil of mist now shrouds that face
No smile, no laugh a slower pace
The marriage now is at an end
It would appear it will not mend.

Her Royal Highness, she is no more
But still she's loved by rich and poor
Now she's Diana Princess of Wales
She's free to seek out other males.

At last she finds a real good friend
Her heart can now, start to mend
That laughing smiling face is back
As they are hounded by a paparazzi pack.

On an early August morning
Di meets death, there was no warning
Into a tunnel dark and black
Her car flips over on it's back.

Now a nation deep in mourning
Flowers, prayers, yes it's dawning
Diana Princess is no more
As she enters through, heaven's door

Farewell my Princess, you were the best
I pray for you as you're laid to rest
I promise that, I shall not weep
As your body lies in the ground so deep.

Ray Jacks

In Memory Of Diana, The Princess Of Wales

May your golden smile and heart.
Light our darkest path.
For the lost, sick, and homeless,
God bless, our people's Queen from the people
Who loved her dearly. . .

Diane Godbold

Queen Of Hearts

The Queen of Hearts you've gone forever,
To everyone's surprise,
No-one could believe the news,
Nearly everyone cried,
Those who never shed a tear,
Mourned in a different way,
Everyone showed some respect,
By giving flowers for your grave,
No-one will forget you,
Your love for the world was strong,
You made everyone feel special,
As if they could do no wrong,
Princess Diana why did you go,
The world needs your special kind of glow.

Marie Evans

Diana

(She was a very special Lady, who will be greatly missed.)

Like a rosebud, small and shy,
You raised your head and faced the world,
The bud it bloomed and showed its colour,
A delicate beauty for all to behold,
The bloom so open, so full of life,
Touched the world with tenderness,
But just when the rose was at its most radiant,
Along they came and cut it down,
Its life extinguished, just like a flame,
Never, ever to bloom again.

Tina Elener

All We Had

You lived. You loved. You cared. We lost.
Media. News Pictures Cost.
Natural love. Mother Earth.
Ambassador. A World of Worth.

You took the stars. You shared them out.
Presented hope. Enlightening doubt.
A fairy tale. A dream come true.
Heart of a Nation. A picture of you.

Your love reached out. Touched with care.
Disfigured lives. Decay. Despair.
Famine. Disease. Relics of War.
Love for these and many more.
The Aged. The Young. Humanities Need.
The World has lost to Inhuman Greed.

Two boys at home, who've lost a mother.
Irreplaceable. Like no other.

Now and Forever you'll always be,
Our 'Queen of Hearts'. Eternally.

Where Jesus walked, Diana went.
Where Jesus Loved, her love she spent.

HRH The World's Princess Diana
1961-1997

Gossamer wings. A pale blue sky
Heaven on Earth. Never Goodbye.

Linda Dickerson

Diana

Shadow lost
life cruelly snatched
death's dark calling

A nation shocked
grieving, weeping
tears are falling

Spirit released
full of shining splendour
a spark of hope

Angel of mercy
illuminating hearts
giving us the will to cope

Your short life
a burning beacon
lifting the gloom

Spreading love
a sea of light
dispelling doom

A catalyst
uniting nations
gathered mourning

Never forgotten
etched in memory
a new age is dawning

*The people's heroine
worshipped woman
of many parts*

*Rest in peace
beloved Diana
Queen of Hearts*

Paul Birkitt

Untitled

*Pavements are the flower bearers
Gun carriage, coffin's throne
For a Queen that never ruled England
Though English hearts she won.*

*A London City standstill
Never seen before
A million mournful faces
Build a city wall.*

*A tribute to a princess
Whose fairy tale died
Extinguished, leaving darkness
A nation knelt and cried.*

Siân Kelly-Scott

Princess Diana

*Like a beacon shining bright,
you turned the darkness into light.*

*Your smile as radiant as the sun,
brightened the hearts of everyone.*

*You blessed us with your caring touch,
and we loved you very much.*

*Then like a snowflake's fleeting stay,
God's angels carried you away.*

*Our lives are poorer without you,
Queen of Hearts, so loving and true.*

*We as a nation shed many tears,
and we'll cherish memories of your short years.*

*I wish I had met you but it was not to be,
for others needed you much more than me.*

*The millions of flowers may fade away
but your youth and beauty forever will stay.*

*You are the brightest star in the sky,
and I hope I meet you in the sweet bye and bye.*

Pamela Eckhardt

A Tribute To Diana, Princess Of Wales

*Diana, Princess of all the people,
Your charm and beauty was so graceful,
The best are taken to live above,
But never forgotten for their love.*

You will now live on within your sons,
You were the greatest of all mums,
Rest in peace with your special friend,
May your happiness now never end.

Angie J Gibbs

Diana, Princess Of Wales

D iana Princess of Wales -
I n each mind a fond memories prevail - of
A heart which was loving and filled people's need -
N o prejudice of colour or creed.
A Princess of beauty, charm and such grace -

P ut sick people at ease with a single embrace -
R eaching out often a kind helping hand - to the
I njured, maimed - who could not stand.
N othing daunted or held her back -
C ourage and energy she did not lack -
E yes so beautiful and blue - witnessed
S ights of what landmines can do.
S uffering humanity she helped without pause -

O pining that banning of mines be the laws.
F un-loving, generous with a lively quick wit

W herever she went a dark corner she lit
A bove and beyond a dutiful call - her deep
L ove for people never ceased to enthral.
E legant, modest - a Lady unique -
S tilled now - her heart - but thro' her works to us speaks.

Marian Curtis Jones

Farewell Princess Of Wales

*A nation mourned the loss,
this sad September day.
Of a star, cruelly extinguished,
to shine, in the Milky Way.*

*This beautiful English Rose,
never meant to grow old.
Whose legend will endure forever.
Because the Lord, broke the mould.*

*Such scenes never before witnessed,
in London's teeming streets.
An overpowering silence,
as the Princess's cortege progressed.*

*Diana's boys, William and Harry,
followed their mother's coffin,
on which a wreath of lilies,
bore the simple word 'Mummy'.*

*Union flag at half-mast,
the palace declares consent.
People Power, the die is cast.
Protocol, uniquely, absent.*

*A horse-drawn carriage,
escorted by Welsh guards and Troopers.
Abbey bells, pealed in homage,
as poignant as the mourners.*

Princess Diana's last journey,
in the flower strewn hearse.
Through silent crowds,
of those she loved.
Remember, the happy nursery nurse.

Raymond Baggaley

Lady Sunshine

Lady Sunshine what has happened to you
You came here with so much to do
Lady Sunshine you were so unaware
Of the evil which lay everywhere

You had a touch of innocence about you
That the tougher kind took in their stride
And as I sit here writing about you
I cannot understand why you have died

For I see so many around taking all they can
They never think of giving a thing
I think you learned a long time ago
Something they may never know
Simply the joy that giving can bring

Lady Sunshine you looked so well
With your beauty and insecurity
There were times when you stumbled and fell
I know it wasn't easy to know life wasn't easy
Princess of our time
Your beauty will live on Lady Sunshine.

Valerie Marshall

Diana

*We saw a chrysalis transform
Into a moth.
Slender
Tender
Resplendent in
Beauty
And frailty.*

*We praised her work
For victims
Of AIDS
Grenades
The underprivileged
The suffering
The dying.*

*We longed to claim her
As our own.
We fought
And bought
Every picture
Indiscreet
And revealing.*

*Now she is dead
Crushed in a car
Slaughtered
And martyred.
Her blood
Is on our hands.
We bought the newspapers.*

Frank Henry

Princess Diana

In the year of nineteen sixty-one
A beautiful baby girl was born
Engaged to your Prince Charming
How you looked a darling
Charming like Cinderella on your marriage
Travelling in a horse and carriage
William and Harry were your boys
Bringing you both happiness and joys
Diana you cared for Dodi with your heart
But far too soon you were to depart
A whole world will remember
That bleak day in September
Diana we have memories to treasure
More than any words can measure

Ann Burton

A Tribute To Diana

An unstoppable tide of tears flowed
As a nation's grief was felt across the land
Its soul, its heart now broken
As tragedy was now at hand
A light once bright
Had now been extinguished from within
As one by one they came remembering a princess
Whose lasting love upon a nation
Had won our hearts.

A W Harvey

May Flowers Grow

May flowers grow,
Colourful, radiant, from ashes below

May they flow,
Freely, lovingly, from head to toe.

Each sombre day, though disbelieved.
Mourning hearts, broken, grieved.

Tears, thoughts, anger come seeping in,
Sorrow, sadness, here within.

We've listened, learned, the people churned.
Young heart and soul, sadly burned.

Explain!
I cannot do.

The Nation was and will, remember You.

Mr & Mrs L Smith

Tribute To Diana

Gap too wide for another to cover
Deep the loss for her sisters and brother
With them the world poured out their grief
Shedding tears of sadness seeking relief

Diana where possible showed kindness and love
He for knowing the Lord God up above
Killer uncaring stole away her young years
Sons with future without mother so dear

Born she was of high standard blood
Faced her enemies for longer than should
Quietly alone she sat in deep sadness
Late her portion of joy with gladness

Diana her name shall not fade away
Of the last day of August what can we say
Stunning she was in all of splendour
Expression of adoration her boys too remember

Hannah Birch

To The People's Princess
(To Diana, Princess of Wales.
May you and Dodi rest in peace. Always to be
remembered forever in our hearts.)

Silence the cameras
Close up the lens
There will be no more pictures of you again
Hold the papers
Let nothing else be said
Now the world knows that you are dead.
Dressed in black
The mourning starts
Pay tribute to the Queen of Hearts
Gone now to a better place
No more intrusions will you face
Farewell from me to England's best
Now finally let the cameras rest.

Anita Farrington

Forever In Our Thoughts
(William and Harry)

We feel your loss
We feel your pain
In grief and sorrow
We extend a wrap of warmth
A sadness has engulfed us all
Man, woman and child alike
To you both our sympathy lies
Words we offer in comfort
Our love and compassion will remain loyal
Be brave, be strong
Our thoughts are with you both always
One may take comfort from the other
May our flowers and cards cushion the pain
We the public share your grief.

Helen Nelson

Princess Diana

You were a special lady, who radiated love
And cheered hearts of those you touched.
Your warm smile and caring personality
Shared with your courage and sincerity,
Earned love and admiration from everybody

But now you have gone to the heavens above
Cruelly taken along with the man you loved.
Our hearts ache for such a tragic loss
A vast raincloud, wet tears of grief,
Releasing sadness, as our eyes openly weep.

Tides of time will hopefully stop the pain
But not the boundless love that we hold,
That shall survive and need not be told.
May you now have peace and eternal rest
Our much missed - 'People's Princess'.

Stephanie Bones

For The Love Of Diana

The heavens wept with us today
There are not words enough for what
                                I need to say.

A downpouring of rain
An outpouring of pain.

Please let the light and warmth
That radiated, permeated
Be enough to lift us all
And inspire us.
For I fear the world is now a darker place.

There are two among us,
Who I hope can feel our love
For their loss is immeasurable,
But I know they carry the same goodness
That will keep her spirit alive

An outpouring of pain
A downpouring of rain

The heavens wept with us today.

Vivienne M Wright

A Burning Candle

A burning candle that burns bright,
giving out light, and spreading knowledge
is truly a magnificent sight.
Over time as it burns slowly,
you can see that the light it gives out is for you,
it's to make your life brighter.
But as this candle completely melts, I think of
only one thing, and that is the bright light that
comes from the candle represents the 17 years of
your life that you gave to our country -
United Kingdom.
The joys of watching people smile and the
sorrow that comes from the world, is enough
to make, anyone think twice about dedicating
their life to help others, so I just want to say . . .
The bright light that you gave out over the
years, will always live in the hearts of those
people you have touched and helped!

Jyoti Patel

Princess Of Smiles And Tears

Diana was a jewel
That shined so bright
She had that distinctive demeanour
Turning darkness into light

There can never be another
No other could take your place
The Queen of Hearts the world over
So alluring and full of grace

You left us oh, so sorrowful
We loved you oh, so dear
Our People's Princess
We all now shed a tear

Forever we will think of you
Time may help ease the pain
God in heaven care for our Diana
Until the time we meet again.

P J Knightly

Diana

(Tribute to Diana Princess of Wales written especially for the Princes William and Harry)

Diana was like a butterfly
She spread her wings and learnt to fly
She fluttered her wings from heart to heart
Bringing love and beauty to worlds apart
With so much love she did much good
Proud to be doing what she could
But much too soon to Heaven she's flown
Leaving us all but not alone
In years to come and you should die
Then off to Heaven you will fly
Who will be waiting at those pearly gates
With arms outstretched and smiling face
Your mother Diana all beauty and grace
To hold you forever in her embrace.

With much sadness and love.

Jean

Just A Short Time

*You came to us in a fairytale way
When you married Prince Charles on your
wedding day.
You wanted your husband to love you so much
It showed in your kiss, it showed in your touch.
Prince William was born how proud we could see
Prince Charles, Princess Diana and William
made three.
You both were still together when Harry
came along
But your feelings were changing, love wasn't
so strong.
You were criticised for speaking, about the pain
that you felt
But that's just how women work, with pain
they've been dealt.
It wasn't that you were cunning, you just
wanted to say
To the people you loved, Charles turned
me away.
The boys both adored you that was plain to see
When you took them both out like a
normal family.
You had so much to do, some days must have
been tough
But you never stopped caring when the going
got rough.
You were looking for love when Dodi came along
He made you feel wanted, was that really
so wrong?*

You'll always be with us, but wherever you are
I hope you're with Dodi, and your Dad's not too far.
At last you're at peace, and as free as a bird
But it's taken your Death, life's really absurd.

Judith Stevens

Farewell To A Princess

She was goodness she was kindness
She was gentle she had love
The good Lord sought to take her
To a new world up above

And because of all the hardships
She faced down here on earth
She was given the chance of staying
Or going forward to re-birth

She chose the later option
And a partner to share it with
And together they're in Heaven
United they both will live

It's a better place they are now
With peace and love and caring
Far from the human beings
That made their lives despairing

No longer can those plague them
That made their lives a hell
Lessons learned, maybe!
We bid you both farewell.

Jean McDonnell

Diana, Always

In our hearts
  in our minds
forever with us
  for all of time.
You were an angel
  a gift from above
you gave us happiness
  and so much love.
You were our saviour
  our hopes and dreams
you will always be
  remembered
for your smile that
  beamed.
You gave so much
  to people everywhere
you really did
  truly care.
You were full of laughter
  full of fun
your heart was as bright
  and as big as the sun.
You were an example
  of how kind we could be
we must carry that on
  now that your spirit
is free.
  But how will we cope
and who will show us the
  way
when you left us
  it darkened our days.

There is a pain
  in our hearts
hurt in our souls
  all we have left
is a big empty hole.
  We won't be the same
now you're not here
  all we are left with
is our sorrowful tears.
  The world will miss you
for the loss of a friend
  I cannot believe it has come
to an end.
  It isn't right
you should be here
  you had so much to give
for so many years.
  You will always be with us
when we look in
  our hearts
but surely this wasn't the
  time
you were meant to part.
  We will miss you
for the rest of all time
  the good that you did
we will keep in our minds.
  You were a Legend
whose life will live on
  because you're not here
doesn't mean that you're gone.
  We will love you forever
and keep every part
  for you are quite simply

Queen of
  Our
    Hearts.

  Diana, Princess of Wales
  You will be missed.
Caroline Amess

A 'Legend' In Her Lifetime

Our Lady Diana, we grieve today.
A nation 'heartbroken' God plucked you away.
Everyone loved you, a beauty to behold
'Lord' carve her name with pride in letters
of 'gold'.

Your 'smile' haunts us forever, a star
shining bright
Our own 'special Princess' hand-in-hand
with her 'knight'.
An ocean of tears, like we've NEVER seen.
An abundance of flowers, NEVER have been.

The world has lost a 'Diva' regardless of
creed or race.
And we have lost an 'Icon' that can NEVER
be replaced
We commend to you this Precious-soul,
For her to achieve her Ultimate Goal.

We pray the world come together as 'One'
Diana's work fulfilled and second to 'None'!
In DEATH she deserves her peace and her rest.
In LIFE dear Lord she was simply 'THE BEST'!

Dilys Parry

August 31st 1997

Today is a day of great sadness
Our Princess Diana has died,
Thousands of people laid flowers
And millions more of them cried.
Her life had been filled with sadness
She married the heir to the throne,
She gave him two wonderful children
But the press couldn't leave her alone.
Princess Diana our Queen of Hearts
Was loved both at home and afar,
Her tireless work for charity
Had made our Princess quite a star.
Her private life was unhappy
Rejected by Charles from the start,
But she had to be strong fro her children
When Prince Charles had broken her heart.
For once in her life she was happy
When Dodi Al Fayed made her smile,
He took her away from her troubles
Where she was content for a while.
When leaving a restaurant in Paris
With Dodi her 'knight' by her side,
And hounded again by photographers
Set out for that last fateful ride.
Our modern day Mother Theresa
Courageous and strong to the end,
Lives on happily high up in heaven
With Dodi, her real special friend.

Nicky Handley

Diana

Diana, the day you died
I feel in some strange way
It was a blessing in disguise
For if you had lived
And Dodi died
I can only imagine the tears
You would have cried.
Now Heaven is holding you
In its arms
Keeping you from all life's harms
No longer will we see
Your beautiful face
But in our hearts
You will always have a place.

Debbie Allen

Together Forever

Two bright stars shine from the night sky
One is Dodi and the other Di
Two smiling faces above the clouds
Now away from photographing crowds
And as they walk hand-in-hand
Across a beach of golden sand
It's such a shame no-one will see
Just how happy Di and Dodi will be
Together forever in eternal rest
Proves that God only takes the best.

Allison Jones

Princess Of The People

Rest in peace our gracious Princess
Your work is over now
They must have missed you up above
We'll meet again somehow

Oh Princess of the people
You passed by us today
All the people they were holding flowers
Which were strewn across your way

And our hearts were filled with sadness
Which we've never known before
Sorrow for your children who have lost
                                        their mother
And we've no Princess anymore

For the length of your procession
You never were alone
Your people adorned your hearse with flowers
All along your route to home

Never be a sadder day in London
For your funeral so many have come
What a cruel reminder we are mortal
But Lord Thy will be done

God bless you our Diana
Your death tore us apart
But you'll always hold a special place
In every person's heart.

Fred Tighe

A Tribute To Diana, Princess Of Wales

*Those years we have known you are endearing
So beautiful so kind
Looked the whole world over but just not find
a Princess such as you
Now grief is on our mind
You were God's messenger always there on call
You grew up and married before hearing
your public call
You have won our hearts Diana even in your
last breath
Nothing takes you from us
Not even the stillness of death
You lived your life at a fast pace and always
beat the clock
Now you have died tragically and we must bear
the shock
We will look to family in our future days
Giving them the love you have shown in so many
different ways
We will watch our every move and discourage
nasty deeds
Remembering your kindness how you thought
of others' needs
Life was not so good for you indeed it was
quite rash
It plummeted you through Paris streets and stole
you in a crash
Family is there for you and friends there are
so many
How fate dealt that twisted blow it really is
uncanny*

*Charles will go on loving the children indeed
he is so caring
He just knows and so do we that you will still
be sharing
Bye Diana too young to sleep - All we can do is
give you flowers before falling down in grief.*

Rosaleen and family

Diana - The People's Princess

*Diana was a princess everyone loved,
now God has seen fit to take her above,
but why take her so young and in her prime?
Surely God, it was not really her time?
There was so much more she could have done,
and what about William and Harry, her
precious sons,
right now they must feel that their lives
are undone,
wondering why God has taken their
precious Mum,
They loved her dearly, that much is true,
so why did you take her God, to be with you,
for once she had found happiness in her life,
and I think Dodi would have taken her for
his wife.
It's such a shame that they should die,
and only you, God, will ever know why.
She as gentle, loving, kind and true,
and now God, she rests with you.*

Anne Adams

Diana - England's Rose

You were great
and you were kind
There's nobody else like you
we could ever find.

You filled people's hearts full of joy,
you could do this to anybody,
it might have been man,
woman, girl or boy.

You could brighten and lift
people's spirits, through their
illnesses, wounds and pains,
just by talking to them or calling their names.

Diana, you had a special talent that
nobody else had,
I'm sure you made people very happy
and very glad.

But now it is so sad, that you have to die,
and so we have to say
farewell Diana, and goodbye.

So, last of all, I have to thank you
Diana, for what you have done on earth
and I have to say, you have been the kindest,
most wonderful woman since your birth.

Jamie Redding (12)

The Passing Of A Princess

*I woke up on Sunday
And they said that you had gone
I just couldn't believe it
It's so terribly wrong.*

*I read in the paper
The real awful truth
And saw from the pictures
The heart-wrenching proof.*

*I'm so sorry Diana
That your life had to end
You were a saviour to us all
A true loyal friend.*

*Our hearts are all broken
And deeply distressed
Because you were so wonderful
Just simply the best.*

*So now you're in heaven
With Dodi your friend
I wish you both eternal happiness
That will never end.*

*Now your beautiful face
We will never see again
It has left us all crying
And so full of pain.*

*So rest now sweet Princess
Your memory lives on
We will never forget you
Even though you have gone.*

Gary Long

Diana, Princess Of Wales
1961-1997

She came upon the scene with a shy coy look
in her eyes,
The radiance of her smile took everyone
by surprise,
The freshness of her youth with her
determined ways,
Revitalised the Royals through out all her days,
The love in her heart was there for everyone,
Not just her sons saw her full of fun,
She had compassion, for people on the street,
Each heart was touched with love, by people
she did meet,
Her work for Charities, The Homeless and those
with AIDS,
Gave others hope and love in many
different ways,
She had her own struggles and even faced
divorce,
Yet she carried on and did things by choice,
Her work to abolish landmines and the damage
they bring,
Gave everyone a new prospective - she was
inspiring,
She was England's greatest ambassador and
countries from abroad,
Took her in their hearts and lingered on
her words,
Yes she had style and grace with a warm look
in her eye,

*She was the Queen of Hearts - yet I'm wondering
why,
Why she wasn't given privacy in her private life
as she pleaded for,
She was constantly in camera - often by
the score,
When you give so much love and friendship -
was it too much to ask,
For a few minutes peace and quiet to get on
with your task,
And now she's gently sleeping safe in God's
good care,
Gently protected, Unique, and so very rare.*

Christine Helen Cruse

Queen Of Hearts

*Princess Diana, Queen of Hearts
A human being, a mother like most of us,
You did us proud, you stood up for your rights
You did not give in, you held on tight.
Your heart ruled for your children and
the world,
Many a hand you held.
Pleasure, comfort to the needy you gave
Happy you made them with your smiles
or a wave
Never to be forgotten, in our hearts
you will stay
You have shown us the light of day.*

Maria Smith

Princess Diana

*She's my inspiration to be a hero.
If we all could be like her
The world would never fall apart.
If everybody did some charity deed
The world would pull together to be one.*

*One day I'll cry a tear for you, my dear.
Today I am too shocked to know the full.
It's not just me to suffer, England alone,
But the whole Nation.*

*What is the world going to be without you?
Nobody knows.
If only we could share that last moment together,
Just to show exactly how much I care about you.*

*I wish I could have met you as you are my
                                    inspiration.
You were the one to break down the barriers
Between old and young, sick and dying.
You were never above the rest
But shed a tear when sorrow affected
You were the only one to care about all.*

*Not only were you an inspiration to me,
                        but to others too.
How are we to cope with no Patron Saint
        of so many charities and sufferers?*

Who shall take your role as the only one to care?

*Rest in peace
As we all remember the good things you did,
And hope to continue.*

You were a hero to the Nation
A carer, a friend, a mother - but few to name.
You shall be sadly missed.
But most of all you were an inspiration,
A hero to remain.

Samantha Malster

Diana
Queen Of Hearts

On 6th September 1997
Is when our Princess went up to heaven
Up in the sky her star will glitter
Leaving many below feeling angry and bitter
Why do you take the beautiful ones?
Leaving behind two heartbroken sons
She was so full of life, too young to depart
To us she was the Queen of Hearts
No-one will ever take her place
Such a caring Lady such a beautiful face
A daughter, a sister, a mother, a wife
She did so much good, in her short life
The Nation's in mourning, under a cloud
Princes William and Harry stood regal
and proud
They can't understand why she had to die
Only in private do they sit and cry
Forever her memory will linger on
Although in our hearts we know she has gone
To a far better place up in the sky
God bless you and keep you Princess Di.

Sue Hamilton

Diana

*From that clay
there came no sign.
Almost a child
and enjoying
the flattery of photos,
the hugs of children
the laughter
of true friends.
Changing with the years
as springtime wife
a baby breeder
then unrequired
thrust into suffering.
Reactions all askew
staircase falls
Bulimia
and careless men.
Claustrophobic
you burst
outwards to hold
the broken child
to touch the AIDS stricken.
Nursing the legless one
of selfish wars,
the Christ missed children
you though scorned
and hounded,
you from naive clay
surprised us all.*

Death in a flash
came too soon
but now peace
a nation holds your hand.

Alan Graham

Hug

Gone now
I feel only sorrow
Concern
For your children
For their tomorrow
You would not wish
Anyone to hate
Or retaliate
With a simple hug
You showed how easy
It is to love
To forgive
You were not perfect
You did not hide
In a pretentious world
You walked amongst us
A Queen disguised as a Princess
Gaining back the love you showed
Tenfold
Not knowing you were
Our special shining star
Diana, Princess of Wales.

J Robson

Dear Diana

Dear Diana you gave so much
You seemed to have the magic touch
Your eyes so blue and full of light
Your smile made a grey day bright

You cared about other people
Less fortunate than you
People with AIDS the poor
Children, these are just a few

But sadly your life came
To an abrupt end
The world lost the people's friend
But although you may be gone
Your spirit lives on

So don't be blue, but carry on
All Diana's good work will be done
And give William and Harry too
The strength and courage to start anew.

J Pearson

Diana

Diana our bright and shining star,
The people's own beloved queen,
We thought nothing could mar,
What has now become a dream.

For in our hearts you'll always stay,
Forever shining through,
And whatever comes our way,
We always will love you.

We know that life must go on,
Though our love will never cease,
And now that you are gone,
Diana rest in peace.

Sheila E McMillan

A Friend Of Friends

A heart so very heavy
With love and interpretation
For those that were reached out to,
In many different ways

No matter what the suffering
A helping hand, and a cuddle
Wasn't far away when needed
To ease a plight of compassion

From one side of the globe to the other,
The work was never-ending,
But oh, what pleasure it brought
In helping different charities along the way.

This life is now no more
Laid to rest in God's Kingdom
With lots left still to achieve,
But sadly, cannot be completed

All our memories will linger
For a Princess dearly missed,
And maybe through the following years
Will we come to terms with our loss.

S J Davidson

Diana

*My tribute to Princess Diana is in praise
of her warm human side,
In dealing with sick children, Diana let her
heart be her guide,
Her hugs, were a legion, as was sitting
on her knee,
Comfort was passed by a handshake, I think
you will agree,
I did admire her courage, when let down by
so-called friends,
Those hurtful remarks remembered, to her
journey's end,
Princess Diana, was a loose cannon,
a dangerous woman I recall,
No-one jumped in to defend her, last of all
the Royals,
When Princess Diana, was going through
a bad patch all sorts of rumours grew,
But Diana, in a witty speech said, her head
was not down the loo!
Princess Diana's greatest treasures, was not
a glittering tiara, or a sparkling diamond ring,
No, her greatest treasures, were
Prince William and Prince Harry with their
boyish grins,
The hush of the crowds, the applause, with
flowers being thrown on the hearse,
This is unusual, or perhaps a new trend,
this is Britain at its best,
Princess Diana was beautiful, had charm, and
dress sense, with style of her own,
No wonder those flowers kept arriving as soon
as her death was known,*

God gave peace, Princess Diana, you are
now and forever in his care,
Buried on an island, your family's choice
away from the camera's glare!
Special flowers had a card that said 'Mummy'
as on her coffin they lay,
Their sad tribute to Diana, and
Prince William and Prince Harry's worst day,
So who's sorry now? Who back-pedalled
when they saw the tributes of flowers laid down
Who's sorry now?:

Dinah Matthew

Our Princess

To our Princess, a devoted Mother
Your first priority, wherever you might be.
Our Princess, you loved your sons above all other,
That was plain for us all to see.

Your smile and devotion spread far and wide,
Our Princess you spread your warmth around,
When problems engulfed you, you did not run
                                    and hide
Another visit to the needy, a comfort in this
                                    you found.

Our Princess you are now in heaven above,
Leaving us feeling empty and blue,
But we will smile and remember your love
Queen of Hearts, Our Princess, we will miss you.

Margaret Phillips

Diana

Light shining like a star
People you touched, felt your warmth

You a giver not a taker
Maker of dreams you made them come true

High or low, always you inquired
Wanted to know, caring

Light's gone out
You've faded away

Someone's selfishness
Makes the words hard to say

You so young, leaving sons
A Nation grieves, sorrow is their tomorrows

You touched millions, with your leaving
Song written about you, words happy and sad

You with the smile, pleasant with your presence
Somehow had to leave and go to heaven.

Dennis Turner

A Moment To Live
(In Tribute To Diana Princess of Wales)

It is for a moment . . .
we live,
It may seem longer . . .
but no!
Time passes by so quick,
No time to forgive,

So take a look at life,
Before it passes you by,
No longer on earth,
But in Heaven above the sky.

Jessica Wright

Princess In The Sky
(Diana's final goodbye)

The light behind the stars I'll be
Forever young, bright and free,
Not black and white or from afar
Instead I'll shine like a bright new star.

And in my own true light I will gleam
Not from a front page or on a screen,
And my thoughts and feelings will be my own
Not the right of a camera lens or microphone.

Up here I'll feel no need to ever hide
And I'll have Dodi right by my side,
So please dry your tears, don't cry and mourn
For I've been given the chance to be reborn.

God's issued me with my final break
A gift I feel in my heart, I must take,
Family and friends I'll miss and leave a
memory of love,
And for my sons I'll forever be an inner
voice from above.

So do not view it as a tragedy for me to die,
For I can now be a Princess in the sky.

Vicky Dillingham

The People's Princess

Sunday morning the people cry,
The news flash said we've lost poor Di.
Her short blond hair and eyes of blue.
The Country of England don't know
what to do.

Killed in a car crash on their way home.
Diana and Dodi were not alone.
The love they had no-one could have more.
The paparazzi closed their door.

Poor William and Harry heard Charlie say.
'My grown up boys Mummy's gone away'
She adored her boys from head to toe.
Our sweet Diana why did you go?

You worked so hard for your charities.
Everyone worshipped you, they fell to
their knees,
Why did our God take you away,
William and Harry have so much to say.

We'll miss you Di with all our heart.
Your memory and us will never part.
'Cos every day we'll think of you,
William and Harry of them too.

We said goodbye on Saturday,
The black limousine drove you away.
A place of rest you are today.
Your own little island far away.

No more photos will they get of you,
They'll leave you alone, what you asked them
to do.
So rest in peace our sweet Princess,
Your memory lives on, you were the best.

M Craven

Angel

Diana, you were taken from us
While still in your prime
We never said a proper goodbye
Before you were gone, forever this time.

But you gave us two special people
Your pride and joy, your two sons
And in your memory we will look
After them as you would have done.

For you gave the ordinary people
Love which meant so much
You were a Royal Princess
Who had the human touch.

Heaven reclaimed the angel
It had given us in 1961
An angel full of warmth and love
And always full of fun.

The world will always be a much
Sadder place without you near
Although your body is in Heaven
Your spirit will always be here.

Ian Fowler

Lady Di

*A gun carriage rolled through a sea of tears
Shed by millions, on either side of
its procession
A week before our Lady riddled with fear
Left us in awe; proving there is no exception.*

*Death pulls on every wrist, as our sands
run out
And God plucked love, just like the last rose
Ghost fingers of the inevitable had chosen
their night
But our Lady will shine, wherever love blows.*

*Heaven will make a better avenue of
resting place
A place where our media, cannot knock twice
Where the archangels hover, leaving no trace
Of human quilt; which to them mere mice.*

*Don't cry Lady Di, your fears are cradled
by us
Your Princes shall grow, and reflect through
your majesty
Time will heal all for them, although
they'll cuss
But be proud with this world to have shared
in your destiny.*

Goodbye England's Rose, alone at last
in peace
May your spirit mingle, with the
brightest saints
A globe has mourned; now it shall blow kiss
Toward your sacred island, where whispers
are Heaven sent.

George Livingston Shand

A Tribute To The Late Diana, Princess of Wales 1961-1997

Darling Diana, you were loved by all
So young and pure, a sweet young girl
Pomp and Regality became your life
When Charles, Prince of Wales took you
for his wife
Life was not easy and as time went on
You had two sons, a loving mum
You became the focus of attention
With difficulties not to mention
Your work here on Earth must be done
Love and care you showed to everyone
God gave you the courage to bounce back
from your sorrows
With strength to go on and face
your tomorrows
A wonderful Lady, however oppressed
You never gave in - you did your best
You will be remembered with pride and love
As you rest in peace in your home above.

Evelyn A Evans

Compassion Lost

*My heart bleeds for an angel past
And flags the world over fly at half-mast
For faces sad and tears that fall
Like rain down cheeks both large and small
For hearts that ache and throats turned dry
And people saying why, oh why
For days turned grey as voices say
'Diana we love you so'
When no-one cared a toss, good seed
did you sow
So gently did you do God's work ever humble
to a fault
You used your station and position over
obstacles to vault
Your voice your smile worked wonders to
enhance the sick on earth
From heaven you came I'm sure into your
Royal birth
Now sadly gone but not forgot and never
could you be
You had to go this World to show
TO CARE is to be free.*

John Bryan

Diana, Our Princess Of Wales

*A friendly smile, a warm embrace,
A loving Mum, a beautiful face,
And on this day the sunshine beams
As you sail away to your Isle of Dreams.*

Sandra Sharp

To Diana

Our very first Princess of Wales,
Your name will live on from beyond the grave,
Because to us you were always so brave,
Someone so good, someone so kind,
Someone like you is hard to find,
The people loved you your family too,
Everyone who was in contact with you,
You were a Princess, a friend and a mother,
For to us there will never be another,
And Lady Diana you were a first Lady,
Always helpful and kind to the sick
and the needy,
And you, our Princess, though we never met,
When you spoke to us our hearts they
would melt,
But now for us our Princess has gone,
What can we do, can the world go on?
The world at a standstill, the grieving
the same,
At a wonderful person, Diana by name,
But all is not gone, all is not lost,
We'll love you forever, whatever the cost,
And now Diana as you rest in peace,
On your special island - a beautiful place,
And maybe someday when our journey
will end,
Our lovely Diana, with the Angels descend,
'Tis there we will find our Princess above,
Waiting for us, she'll shower us in love.

Iris McFarland

Diana - Queen Of Hearts

*She was the most beautiful woman the world's
ever seen,
A woman one day we hoped would reign as
our Queen,
though a truly loved Princess in our hearts
we could see,
That this woman as Queen was never to be.*

*But how did we know then the fate that was
to befall,
That in her young years she would be snatched
from us all,
That the heart that she gave in so many ways,
Would stop beating for her on that one
fateful day.*

*From the innocent young girl she gained
worldly acclaim,
She married her Prince and took on his name,
She gave him the son that one day would
be King,
She gave her all to his life, she
gave everything.*

*But dark clouds were looming and pressures
too hard to bear,
And the love in her life was no longer there,
But the load on her shoulders she knew she
could carry,
For her much adored sons, Princes William
and Harry.*

*So she travelled the world across seas,
across land,*

*Helped the children and sick by the touch of
her hand,
With warmth and affection she would brighten their day,
And give a bit of herself in her own
special way.
But God knew that this was a woman he could
help from above,
And in his good wisdom gave her a man for
friendship and love,
And for that very short time she was happy
and free,
Her happiness glowing for the whole world
to see.*

*But still she was hounded for that
updated news,
No-one heeded her pleas or respected
her views,
So are we all a little guilty and partly
to blame,
For taking her life and exploiting her fame.*

*Now from life into death she is laid down
to rest,
For the world, for her family she just did
her best,
And we hope that in Heaven her soul she's
now sharing,
With someone she loved who is tender
and caring.*

*So let's pause for a moment and think for
a while,*

> *Remembering her beauty, her caring,*
> *her smile,*
> *And the role that she played in so many parts,*
> *To remember her truly, as our own*
> *'Queen of Hearts'.*

Josephine Giles

Diana

Something so precious has been taken away,
it happened in a sad and awful way.
You are greatly loved and we'll all miss you,
you'll be watching us all especially your two.

You did a lot for the world and not everyone knew then,
Just how special you were rather like a mother hen.
My thoughts and thousands of others are with your two sons,
They will be without the love and the arm of their mums.

Thank you for giving all the love that you gave out,
People are all thankful without a doubt.
You're the People's Princess Lady Diana,
The Queen of our hearts forever.

We love you and miss you.

Marie O'Kane

Tribute To Diana

How great a woman
Could walk on earth.
An angelic smile, with divine beauty.
Kind and thoughtful.
An angel in disguise.
Caressing the sick, to give them hope
Giving them love, for what they had lost
An angel we suddenly lost.
The sky darkened, as we shed a tear.
For the tears that we shed
A stream of flowers, began to appear.
Flooding the land, from end to end,
With a heavenly scent.
The stars above
Shall become, eternal flames
Burning the dark sky, into light.
Hearts begin to bleed.
As she's laid to rest
God bless her soul
For ours, she once blessed
Her name, we shall not forget
As it's carved, deep in our hearts.
With elegance and harmony.
The choirs sing, as people pray.
Remembering an angel.
For whom, her name, we'll remember.
DIANA.

Richard Wolfendale

We Came From Miles Around

*We came from miles around,
'Your funeral was great!'
The message in our feelings attempting
to relate;
Our love for you,
Our hate for them
How strong emotions were.*

*The sky has picked a rose today;
This country's finest flower.*

*But where had all this started,
In England's finest hour?
You didn't hold the wheel then,
it wasn't in your power.*

*Always an outsider, always one of us,
reaching to the heights and hearts,
that others could not touch.*

*The people won't forget you
your life was not in vain
in Heaven as on Earth,
ever to remain.*

*Of all the pledges made this day,
your brother held the word.
When any other statement,
would have seemed absurd.*

You've died and gone to Heaven,
of this we can be sure.

But which way up Heaven is,
we'll never know,
no more.

Philip Isle

Diana - The Legend

Most caring person who ever lived,
Diana our best friend,
Now lay in tranquillity,
The legend will never end.

We thank thee Lord for Diana,
Who held the world in her arms,
Helping those in need,
And using her great charms.

Her warmth always surrounded us,
And never would let go,
Even in the darkest nights,
Diana's love would glow.

Those people whom you met,
You'd be utmost in their mind,
Remembered for your smiles,
And for being ever kind.

We all say farewell,
As our beloved Diana departs,
YOU achieved what you wanted,
You are the Queen of Hearts.

Christopher Downs (13)

Diana

A Rose
Whose petals
Will never
Wither
A Rose
Whose scent
Remains
Forever
A light
But hidden
From view
Who shines
Brighter
Now
Than ever
Somewhere
In Eden
The only place
For a rare gem.

Simone Ryder

A Dark September Day

They filled the streets of London,
Two million or more,
A nation sharing in its grief,
As never known before.

For she the lonely bell did toll,
The hollow click of hoof.

So near and yet so far away,
We did gaze in disbelief,
At the power of love and touching,
Of a gentle life so brief.

But she beyond this sombre day,
Will always twinkle bright,
Forever she the Princess,
Who turned darkness into light.

Ken Lowe

Our English Rose

An English Rose, as you were known
A perfect bud, had not yet grown
The sweetest scent upon your face
A loving smile - to any race,
The kindest colour, was in your heart
An eternal glow that won't depart
The warmest person one could know
Who made the hearts of many glow,
No riddled cancer - to you, seemed fair
For in your arms your cradle care
No saddened child you'd turn away
But hold them in a loving way
A memory true to any soul
To aim and reach their highest goal
No-one was lowly - not to you
A smile a tear would shine on through
An English Rose, that is no more
Beheld your heart forever more
This country that will mourn for thee
But oh Diana - now, you are free!

Fiona Gilpin

Diana

Gentle Lady, whose love and affection,
Has captured the world.
Leaving humanity, speechless by,
Your premature and unwarranted demise;
Numbed and saddened to a degree unknown
by many,
Your absence has, united the world in sorrow,
Leaving people thinking hard as to why?
These dreadful things need happen.
An emptiness and a great Miss-you-ness,
Overshadows each one of us at this time.
Unable to comprehend the reasons as to why,
You were snatched away from us too soon.
Recalling your radiant smile,
The sparkle in those beautiful blue eyes,
We cry, realising we shall see them no more;
Touched by your unceasing concern for the
sick and needy,
Remembering how many people you brought
new hope to.
You always gave all of yourself during
these times,
We can only be thankful for the years you
graced our world,
Even though we wish with all our hearts,
it could have been for longer.

*Still in your tender years, such a perfect
image to behold;
Both externally and internally,
Unforgettable, 'Sweet Princess' you will
remain in our hearts,
Remembered always for your tender,
loving touch.*

Amanda-Lea Manning

In Memory Of Diana, Princess of Wales

I'd like to be a mender
of all the broken hearts

I'd like to be a seamstress who
sews the things in life that
fall apart

I'd like to give smiles to those
who have no fun
I'd like to be a refuge into which
they could run

I'd like to be the water
in a dreaded drought
I'd like to have a heart
in which you'd find no doubt

I'd like to reach my hand out
for those who are about to fall
There's not one thing I'd like to be . . .
I'd like to be them all . . .

Lorraine Day

Diana, Princess Of Wales

*Dear Princess Di, the world and I
will mourn your loss, and wonder,
Whose fateful hand destroyed your life,
And tore our heart asunder.*

*No words of mine, however fine,
Could enhance your charm, and beauty,
The love and tenderness you displayed,
Outshone the light, of duty.*

*This nation's grief, will not be brief,
Though time may ease the pain,
For a nation's tears, will outlive the years,
At the mention of your name.*

*Your memory will live, for evermore,
In the hearts of the needy, and the poor,
Those were the ones, who day by day,
Heard your message, heard you say.*

*Give out more love, and end the pain,
We will not see your like again.
But as sure as there's a heaven above,
There you will find peace and love.*

Edna Hunt

God Lent Us An Angel

God lent us an Angel,
Diana was her name,
Then one day he took her back,
To Heaven from whence she came.

Her love and warmth lit up our world,
Her smiles and charm shone through,
Diana was the Queen of Hearts,
Our love for her just grew.

We never thought she'd leave us,
God only takes the best,
Diana how we miss you,
Now you're laid to rest.

God's taken back his Angel,
We're left behind to grieve,
A nation that's in mourning,
Why did she have to leave?

The thirty-first of August,
Will always spring to mind,
It was the day Diana left us,
This world she left behind.

We'll always remember our Diana,
She's in our thoughts to stay,
Sleeping in a better place,
God bless, sleep tight, we pray.

Amen

Susan May Downs

Final Journey Of A Princess

A heart-warm sea of emerald and cerulean
                               flowers
Surged hard against cliffs of rock-cold faces,
Thawing hard-frozen facades,
Drawing salt water from grief-stricken stone.

The bloom-scented air,
Loaded thick with bursting silence,
Weighed down with solid sorrow,
Trembled as a southerly wind blew.

And out from the petalled sea,
Floating on waves of white blossoms,
Gently steered by motherly wind,
A golden mermaid came forth.

A red rose river led her northward,
Led her home. And as flowers parted,
A radiance rippled outwards in her wake,
Rippled outwards to cliff faces, halting
                               salty erosion.

And, long after the river had run dry,
Long after the sea-bed had been unveiled
                               to sky's eye,
Long after the southerly wind had breathed
                               its last,
A radiance rippled outwards in her wake.

Bruno D'Itri

Princess

To hear such news that tragic day
A life so sadly snatched away
Time stood still in disbelief
While nations joined to share their grief

A solemn silence filled the air
The whole world wept in true despair
For our Princess was gone forever
Though in our hearts forgotten never

Even though now worlds apart
She's still the Queen of all our hearts
A true Princess one of their kind
Such tender warmth so hard to find

As time goes on and tries to heal
The emptiness and pain we feel
We'll think of her in celebration
With love for all her dedication

Though out of sight not out of mind
Sometimes this life is so unkind
A life we proudly once embraced
Now can never be replaced

Goodbye Diana, Princess of Wales.

Lindsey Newrick

We Are Numb

You have been dead but a few brief weeks
*   and we are numb.*
Thoughts of you unbidden come
Of how you were so short a time ago.
Life and laughter, that happy glow
And loving smile
All ours for just a while.

But we must carry on from day to day,
Press on regardless, as we used to say.
And maybe in our dreams sometime when
We least expect it you might come home again,
To smile and hold our hands
And maybe then our loss we'll understand.

Eileen M Lodge

To Princess Diana

Angel to the sick and suffering,
comforter of those in pain,
loved by everyone who knew you,
shall God give us your like again?
Yours, indeed, an ageless beauty,
reflected in both word and deed,
love, compassion, understanding,
sympathy for those in need!
Let us learn from your example,
though, at first, we don't succeed;
who could possibly replace you?
Follow your unselfish creed?

Noel Egbert Williamson

A Princess - And A Mother

On the sixth day of September
Whole Nations said goodbye
To a mother of two children,
Known to all as Princess Di.

People in their millions
Flocked to the Palace gate,
Hardly able to believe
The cruelty of fate.

To sign books of condolence
They stood and queued for hours.
The love she gave out they returned
With tears, poems and flowers.

And money, to her charities.
Because she was so kind,
In her memory, they will continue
The work she left behind.

In Westminster Abbey,
The words of Saint Francis' prayer,
Told that from sadness she brought joy,
Gave hope where there was despair.

We will remember a Princess
In the years to come.
But, our two young Princes
Will just remember their mum.

Pamela Evans

The People's Princess

Our dear beloved Princess,
Was a very special soul,
She shared the grief of others,
And made it her life's goal,
She touched the hearts of millions,
And held babes in her arms,
Was truly quite unique and kind,
The Nation loved her charms,
Countless thousands paid respect,
To our Princess whom we love,
May God Bless her and her friend,
Now both, in Heaven above,
She wanted to make folks aware,
Of the suffering of many,
Whether we are rich or poor,
Or don't possess a penny,
It did not matter to this child,
Her kindness was a light,
That radiated from her heart,
And helped make this world bright,
So I make this a tribute,
To our Regal Princess Di,
You touched so many people,
With that sparkle in your eye,
Prince William and Prince Harry,
Are her two sons she adored,
May they follow in her footsteps,
With that love she always poured,
Then the Nation will stand by them,
And will love them like their Mum,

May God help them feel her presence,
For she'll always be their chum,
I pray that those two children,
Will be strong and will possess,
The courage of their Mother,
Who was a loving, kind, Princess.

Janette Campbell

Diana - Princess Of Wales

What sad news as dawn breaks today.
The world grieves for our lovely
Princess Diana.
Hearts broken, tears falling,
bewilderment too.
Why should she be taken in this
tragic manner?

For one who has helped and encouraged
so many,
She has been dealt a blow, she could
never deserve.
Princess of the people, loved the world over.
Severed from life in her springtime, her gift
was to serve.

Her humility shone through like a beacon,
She lit up so many lives on her way.
Forever in our memories, Diana -
Queen of Hearts.
It is for her special family and loved ones
we pray.

Gwyneth Cleworth

A Fond Farewell To Our Queen Of Hearts

The nation awoke with a painful thunderbolt
Realisation was too far away as numbness
                              filled our senses.
As the news broke:
'Diana, Princess of Wales is Dead'.
We knew this was a cruel lie,
The people did not have a Princess of Wales;
We had a Queen of Hearts
And we knew our Queen could not be dead.

But the truth became ever apparent
As the flowers of hope poured into
                              Kensington Palace.
A united hope that she is happy now,
A dream the nation must share forever;
That Diana; Queen of the People is at last,
Where and with whom she wants to be.
We cannot deny; the end was all too tragic,
But we must believe in sweet Destiny.
We must hope and pray our Queen is now free.

They may have stripped her of the HRH title,
But to the people; to the country;
Diana was above and beyond royalty.
For she knew how to communicate,
How to care, how to love - how to make
                              things happen.
Some say Diana was alienated from the
                              Royal Family,
I think the nation believes this too.

In reality; there will never be another Diana.
Farewell Queen of Hearts - You did make
                                a difference.
With love; Your family of millions. x x x

Matt Valentine

A Princess, An Angel, A Friend

Diana, was an Angel
Sent from God above,
She was the one, who helped the world,
And whom, we love so much.

She taught us, to be good,
She helped, when times were bad,
She was there for everyone,
For this we're all so glad.

Diana, still an Angel
Is in the skies above,
There she can see all of us,
And still give out her love.

Because of our Diana
I know that I have learned
To give, and to be kind.
And all the people, around the world
May have these words in mind.

To our dear Diana may you
Rest in peace. Amen.

S Kirkley

Peace, Love And Diana
(Dedicated in loving memory for Diana,
Princess of the people Queen of our hearts)

Thank you God from high above
For creating Diana for us to love
You picked her out from all the rest
Because you knew we'd love her best

Her gentle touch that gave us hope
Her courage showed us how to cope
She tried to help us where she could
She cared for us, she understood

You knew the joys that she would bring
She made us laugh and cry and sing!
Compassion that she'd never hide
Whenever she was by our side

Beauty that no Rose could touch
We loved Diana very much
Her smile that once lit up the room
Leaves a nation, now in gloom

Our Queen of Hearts she'll always be
Remembered for eternity
For watching us where once she'd been
A golden Angel stands, serene.

Nikki George

A Tribute To A Princess

The suffering and pain which we all feel,
We ask ourselves will it ever heal?

The loss of a Princess which we all have
to bear,
Our Queen of Hearts you really did care.

The outcome of this tragedy leaves us sad and
broken-hearted,
You were too young to leave us Di, your life
had barely started.

Your life an inspiration but so tragically short,
A reason for this death in our minds we've
all sought.

Your need to live in peace, well what can
we say?
God took you for a happier life to a place
far away.

We have to come to terms in the time which
we bide,
While we know you are safe at
Our Father's side.

This poem, a gesture to you which I send,
Your life beautiful Princess, did it really
have to end?

Jayne M Lysyj (15)

A Poet's Homage To Princess Diana

*In the early hours of Sunday morning,
31st August 1997 a Nation's heart was
torn apart, as Princess Diana was tragically
killed. A great, great, loss, leaving people
unbelieving stunned and shocked, who would
show a bereavement never again to be
repeated and recorded in British history.*

*As a World War Two battle hardened
Infantry veteran, I never cared for Royalty.
So what makes an ordinary man like me,
forsake his usual Saturday morning beer,
stay at home and shed a tear?*

*Did a Nation deserve one so dear?
How can humans sink so low to seek
and photo some intimate times of our
Princess without compassion or fear?*

*The Tabloid newspapers who in your short life
hounded and did their utmost to find and print
what they considered the worst of you.
On your death, tried to atone and print the
very best of you.*

*The millions of ordinary people, who never
realised you were part of their family until
you died. They paid their deep respect,
watched you go, and cried. Throwing their
flowers on the passing hearse, with a love
so deep, to a Rose, who's allas so fast asleep.*

Being human we will forget our Diana for periods of time, but to forget you forever, Impossible! The mention or sight of the words, Leprosy or AIDS, will instantly trigger off a mental image of Princess Diana holding the hands of the victims of AIDS or Leprosy, providing a powerful weapon against people's ignorance and fear. Then a tear will appear at the corner of our eye, and future generations should know the simple answer, why.

Princess Diana seemed to draw on a powerful inner strength that her unhappiness appeared to give her, which ignited a bravery few of us ever acquired, enabling her to impart a love to the less fortunate in our society, of which the compassionate people in the world very much admired.

Tom Bull

Vocation

*They tried to constrain me
But my dance sprang from within,
Propelling, impelling me to reach out to
                              the other,
Stretching and expanding the limits of heart
                              and soul,
Embracing, enfolding, and finally encompassing
Suffering humanity across the world.*

Glenna Towler

Princess Diana

Diana was a lovely girl,
Her last weeks she spent in a whirl.
Prince Charles never loved her from the start
That's one of the reasons for deciding to part.
In her marriage there wasn't much joy
Only when she gave birth to each boy.
Her sons will feel grief and pain
But they are young and will live again.
She showed her sons the other way of life
How others live through trouble and strife.
She hoped one day when 'Wills' was King
Things she taught him would mean something.
She was good and showed kindness true
Spent time with the crippled, sick and
homeless too.

Doing it alone how she planned
Trying hard to get landmines banned.
Pictures taken and gowns she wore,
She fitted the name Princess more and more.

It was a terrible and tragic way
How her end came, that awful day.
Nations were shocked and full of tears
This day will be remembered for many years
For Diana was loved by almost everyone
And won't be forgotten now she's gone.
The good die young so they say
But sad as it is, God has just had his way.

The sun shone down with no sign of showers
And no-one has ever seen so many flowers.
As we watched your coffin go slowly by
We had no tears left so we couldn't cry.
People lined your path from beginning to end
Everyone there was saying goodbye
to a friend.
And as you passed there was no sound
Diana, and both your boys did you proud.

Your brother in tribute to you
Let his true feelings come boldly through.
His thoughts and what he said surely will be
Written to go down in history.
Back home and which is for the best
Your body has now been laid to rest,
In surroundings so beautiful and serene,
It's surely the fit place for the people's Queen.

Gwen Smith

Fond Memories Of Diana, Princess Of Wales (1961-1997)

Her smile, so bright, 'neath sparkling blue eyes.
Warm greetings, hugs and gestures keen.
Love and compassion evoking sighs
From the strong, or faithless their
God unseen.

Diana sought-out and conquered evil all.
Children, too, recognised her special Grace.
Fame and glory disdained them, she.
Her sacrifice upheld an Angelic face.

Brian Harris

Our Eternal - The Princess Diana

She walked like a model,
And smiled like a friend,
She was beauty itself,
A new Royal 'trend'.

She had the grace of a Queen,
And the style of a star,
Charisma and charm
A bodyguard and car.

A life full of sadness,
But her heart full of hope,
We loved 'Our Diana',
She showed she could cope.

Diana showed us so much,
How to fight with your heart,
How to share all your love,
How to have a new start.

Her strength was admired,
Her beauty adored,
Her bravery recognised,
For landmines outlawed.

With a new man in her life,
Di looked happy at last,
Until a Harrods' chauffeur,
Drove a car much too fast.

A fatal crash,
One August night,
Killed our Diana,
And turned out our light.

The whole world was in grief,
At the news she was gone,
But we all know in our hearts,
Her memory lives on.

Olivia Lambeth

To Diana

It was such a sad
And tragic day
When God sent his Angels
And took you away
He saw you were tired
And did what he thought best
So he took you to Heaven
Where he knew you could rest

You were the Queen of our hearts
And the strength of our nation
A person so caring
A great inspiration.

A people's Saviour
The sweetest love song
The memory of you
Will always live on.

A bud that never opened
If you only knew
What a difference you made
To this world
And how much this world loved you.

Samantha Jayne Eley

Compassion

*Compassion is a name for love and it's there
within you all,
usually it doesn't surface until you hear an
anguished call,
or sometimes it's in response to a brother
who's in need;
It shouldn't matter who it is, his colour or
his creed.
Because you're all God's children, each sister
and each brother,
the greatest gift you can give to Him, is to
show compassion to each other.
You have had a good example in the child
you called Diana,
She showed a deep compassion in a very
loving manner.
Her love was unconditional, she gave it to all
in need,
to the sick and the homeless, to all warning,
she paid no heed;
she touched the hands of lepers, hugged
victims of AIDS too,
this was to be a lesson, it's what she
came to do.
She broke down many barriers and kept God's
natural law,
because she was who she was, she could open
many a door;
she could show her deep compassion because
she'd also know the pain,
it's easier to understand if you've walked
through showers of rain.*

*Because she did what she did, she's reaping
what she's sown,
compassion keeps just pouring in, from
brethren she's never known.
Gaze at this phenomenon, it's human nature
at its best,
watch it through the coming years, for time
will be its test.
To take on human form and walk upon
your Earth,
means you aren't perfect, your faults are
there from birth.
It was the same with that dear child, but know,
she did her best,
that's all Our Father asks of you, as you come
up against each test.
Make it your responsibility to show
compassion wherever you can,
to nature and to animals, as well as your
fellow man.
You find it very easy to comfort a
distressed child,
but how hard is it to succour your foe,
when he has made you wild?
Sometimes the hardest tests in life make you
feel abused,
you erect a wall around yourself and sit there,
feeling used.
These feelings can turn to selfishness,
compassion can be well covered,
but however deep, it's always there, waiting
to be recovered;*

it's then, when something touches you,
your heart begins to melt,
a wakening to that deep love, for that is
what you've felt.
For some, it is the first time that they've been
moved to pray,
a simple prayer for Diana, is what they came
to say.
Share this deep emotion, do God's work
wherever you can,
extend a hand, a comfort, give love to your
fellow man.
Each show of compassion is personal, some
of you have seen at first hand,
but you have also seen the power when single
acts join as a band.
Never forget this valuable lesson, love's the
greatest power of all,
and whenever the opportunity arises, use the
compassion that's within you all.

Beryl Cosgrave

A Prayer For A Princess

Our Lady,
      You have touched us with your spirit of
grace and love.
Breathed life on us anew;
Freely, you showed us how to give,
In our hour of need, help us to find the strength
to tread in your path and in our own way, make
the World a better place.

Maureen Owen

In Memory . . .

Fragility, yet strength,
Borne from suffering.
Tender empathy,
Exuding compassion.
Joy tinged sadness,
Bearing hope.
Irradiation of life,
Poured out for many.
Intangible beauty,
Beheld in wonder.
Bright dancing sunbeam,
Cast now in shadow.
Cherished in memory,
Through tears with closed eyes.

Graham Wickens

Poetic Tribute To Diana

I loved her looks
I loved her ways
I loved her caring
I loved the days
When in the papers
Her face I would see
Great pleasure and comfort
Would be given to me.
To read the news now
Seems a trifle by far
For the light has gone out
On my favourite Star.

A K Swann

Diana: A Requiem

*Diana was the Goddess of hunting poised
in flight,
And now her modern-day counterpart has
gone to eternal light,
No-one knows what's wrong or right
or what happened that fateful night,
God's ways are not given to us to understand,
Why should He take such an angel; such
a delight,
When the news broke,
I got such a fright,
Like a bolt from the blue, a hideous surprise,
I could feel the tears jolt in my eyes,
Let the funeral bells toll throughout the land,
Surely this was never planned,
One thing for sure,
Diana had allure,
For troubled souls, and rich and poor,
She only had to flash that shy,
beguiling smile,
You were truly the Queen of style,
Ashes to ashes, dust to dust,
You had no-one in whom you could trust,
I went to sign the book of consolation,
To say goodbye from an ever grateful nation,
My sorrow can find no placation,
So from one of humble station,
I write this hymn to you, my pen's creation,
Away from pressman's allegation,
It baffles me,
It must baffle them;*

Now you wear Heaven's diadem,
It must have been one of your dearest joys,
To bring up your beloved boys,
In truth, without you we are not alone,
As long as Prince William sits on
England's throne.

Alan Pow

Our Princess Diana

You were Princess, of Thurnscoe, just for
a day
You were special, like an angel, we wanted
you to stay
laughing, talking freely you showed you cared
a lot
About downtrodden people in a mining
village forgot.
No pit wheel turning, just shops and houses
boarded up
Tin cans and rubbish near your feet but
you didn't even look.
You lit up our grimy village like a
ray of sunshine
In Thurnscoe, for once everything was divine.
You were our Princess, of Thurnscoe, just
for a day
You were special Diana, you've left a
memory that won't fade away.

Lillian Johnson

Glittering Star

Diana a star that shone
And glittered briefly
She came painfully innocent
Into our lives
Pure in heart
Loved complete
But was hurt in return
And found no one could help
Her through those early times
Brought tears to our eyes
When we saw her so sad
With mixtures of emotions
She valiantly fought back
To become maturer and wiser
No one could damage her sweet soul
She befriended the weakest of our race
And left behind a glitter
That had turned to gold
And inherited in the air we breathe.

Vivienne Doncaster

A Young Man's Princess

Although I never met Diana
I felt I knew her so well
And since I was young
She's been in my heart

Beautiful from the first day I saw her
And gorgeous to her last
She graced my young life
Now she'll never leave

I was there to bid farewell to her
My tears ran down London's streets
Along with every man's, woman's and child's
The homeless and our future King's.

The country she brought together
Will remain strong in her name
Just as the world remained silent
To remember and respect her . . .

Gordon S Allen

Diana

A million images frozen in time
couldn't capture the essence of you.
Diana.
The billions of tears shed for loss of your life
can't equate with the grief the world feels.
Diana.
Countless words may be written on whole
                                      forests felled
but they won't express how the world loves you -
Diana.
Our sorrow's intangible - soft as night air
and the fragrance of mountains of flowers.
Diana.
You may now lie alone - but be sure we're
                                        all there.
All hearts bleed . . .
for the Queen of our hearts.
Diana.

Patricia Finney

For A Princess

I behold an angel in a golden sky.
With a halo of love,
She looks down to see
The grand bouquets spread throughout a
grieving world.
She smiles,
Her heart beaming with joy.
She has compassion for those in tears -
She has compassion for those whose ills
She has helped to heal.
A light has departed from the Earth,
But in the heavenly fields a new soul is born.
We know
Her memory will never die.
We know
Her spirit is eternal - shining - at peace . . . .
For evermore.

Keith Barnard

O' Beloved Diana

O Beloved Diana, you outshone
even the brightest of stars. We
will hold you ever dear in our
hearts for you will never fade.

O Angel of grace, charm, kindness
and all good, how we grieve
at our loss unable to bear this
wretched day that lies before us.

O Sweet joy of ours, now you are
in heaven's realm, peaceful at last,
never to be forgotten, evermore to be
cherished.

Samia Chacko

Poem For Remembrance To Diana, Princess Of Wales

With a smile, with the air of grace,
She came into this life to become the
Princess of Wales,
The work she did will be remembered,
The kindness she showed the people
and societies,
The boys she leaves and the future King,
Diana 'Queen of Hearts' has gone but will
not be forgotten,

Hassle, stress, pestering is all they got,
The photographers would not leave her alone,
The face covered worldwide magazines,
the fashion hit the headlines,
The life she had with Prince Charles went
so quickly,
The boys older now, can remember their
mother with all their own personal memories,
William, Harry, and Prince Charles may you
all find peace.

Janet Robinson

Diana

A sweet earthly angel
On a mission of love
Was guided in goodness
By the Lord up above.

A symbol of sainthood
On an errand of hope,
A tutor of love
Showing kind ways to cope.

The people adored her,
The whole world her domain,
Some critics maligned her
And inflicted great pain.

And God's great dilemma
Was to let her remain
Or shield her from heartache
While the world mourns in shame.

Arch Lang

Memories

You only have one Mother
Patient kind and true
No one in this whole wide world
Will be as true as you.

We hold you close
And there you will stay
Within our hearts
To walk with us
Throughout our lives
Until we meet again.

You are still with us
Still in our thoughts
And always in our hearts
But there you only have one mother
Till death do we part.

Janet Brown

Diana The Lady We Love

First a Lady, then a Princess,
To all of us you were the best.
We'll never see one like you again,
You'll always be with us, and with us
you'll reign.
Supreme on high you're not alone,
You sit with God on your Princess' throne,
To watch over us the people you love,
We look to the heavens and know
you're above.

We know you were our Queen of Hearts,
And was dedicated to every part
Of everything that you stood for,
The sick, the homeless and the poor,
You will forever be in our minds,
You found such joy with all mankind.
To have that snatched away from you
In your short life you were good and true.
So goodnight Diana and God bless
You're safe in God's hands and there
you'll rest,
For all of your eternity,
To be at peace and harmony.

Edna Adams

The Bruise-Laden Sky

I think about you and I cry.
I dream about you
and so does the bruise-laden sky.
You at last found true love
and thanked whoever was above.
Together you made a handsome pair
him so dark, you so fair,
but then your happiness was taken away
and we had to face a cold dark day.
Now we walk around with eyes full of tears.
We'll remember you for years and years.
When in secret we have a cry,
we'll think of that cold dark day
when there was a bruise-laden sky.

J M Smith

Portrait Of Diana

Such beauty beyond imagery
captures the eye
Reassures me of love forever
In embracing arms
I hold you so dear

Tears for you
colour my world
As I follow in your footsteps
never to grow old,
And the picture is seen - vividly!

Francis Paul Farnworth

Life Of A Princess

Born in the golden pastures of serenity
Deep in the English countryside
A baby girl became a 'Lady'
Not knowing to what great heights she'd ride
They called the babe 'Diana'
The name of the Goddess of Hunting
Little did they know, that years later
She would wed midst a sea of 'bunting'
Kings and Queens from all over the world
Were present at her wedding
For she had married a Royal son
Her doomed future not suspecting
She gave this man two handsome sons
The people simply adored her
For she was the light in a Palace so dull
But not a Courtier loved her
As years went on her beauty grew
Many hurts and slurs came upon her
Her spirit broke her heart was pained
Her Prince had found another
The world cried out their words of love
Through all her pain and sorrow
But then she found another man
To love her and her boys in the morrow
But in a shocking twist of fate
Life ended for both in a carriage
But Paradise has been given by God
As they received a truly Heavenly marriage.

Moira M Michie

Dear Lord Up Above

Dear Lord up above,
Please open the golden gates
For a very special angel,
An angel so beautiful and kind,
Give her golden wings
To match her heart of gold,
Plant a perfect rose,
With golden petals.
Let it bloom and grow,
Plant it in a special spot.
Don't ever let it die.
Live on forever Diana
As the perfect rose you are,
Bloom on forever Diana
Open up your petals,
Like that golden smile, we all knew.
Please call this rose
'The Golden Angel Rose'.

S Bale

Gentle Diana

Thank you Diana,
You've done a life's work,
so now the Lord has called you home.
They say the good die young!

Gentle Princess,
Madonna to the modern world,
distressed by every cruelty,
distressed by every hurt.

God bless you, Diana,
Princess of Wales,
for all the work you've done to help
the victims in this world.

Gentle Diana,
Queen of all our hearts,
rest you now in splendid state,
but also rest in peace.

Patricia Tilling

Sunday 7th September 1997 'Afternoon'

The sea of people in the Mall
Moved forward to the Palace.
Walking by the scented flowers, piled high
Posies, teddy bears, cards and sprays.
Lighting candles on the way,
Heads of children bent together
Reaching out to lay their wreaths.
All the messages say her name in love
And every photo of her beauty sends
A dart of pain, for they know
We shall ne'er see her face again.
While passing by a tree along the Mall
Its age had seen all sights of pageant,
Through happy times and the sad,
By my feet I heard a sound, - 'plop'!
And looking down I saw a leaf had dropped.
It shimmered, tinted by the delicate hues
*   of autumn.*
I dared not pick it up nor touch its frailty.
The tree had wept and so did I.

Marlene Sarah Jones

The Princess Of The Lake

*Lady Diana Spencer, sweetest rose, home-grown,
was picked by Charles - Heir to the Throne.
She became his wife in a fabulous gown,
and the crowds rejoiced over London town.*

*Sons, the young princess came to bear.
Harry and William, like his mother - fair.
Whilst his wife blossomed out in every way,
the Prince of Wales contrived to stray.*

*Bejewelled and lavishly gowned she went,
beautifying people's lives as if heaven-sent.
A touch, a glance, embrace or smile,
brought the sick and weary hope - awhile.*

*She traversed the world, her all she gave,
performing acts of kindness, so calm and brave.
Stripped of her title, and finally free,
from an adulterous marriage, seeped in acrimony.*

*Dawned the day everyone knew by her glow,
the 'People's Princess' was romancing a beau.
Named - Dodi Al Fayed, of Egyptian blood he,
but dark stars predicted, this love couldn't be.*

*They died together long before their time,
amidst a mangled fusion of metal and grime.
Dressed forever in black, golden hair
                        nowhere grey,
inside leaden coffin, the 'Queen of Hearts' lay.*

*Folks bereaved wept and wailed, extolling her worth.
Flowered shrines grew enmasse upon the
                        sad earth.
Candles burned from shore to shore,
for the angelic one who'd smile no more.*

Now she rests at peace beneath a mound,
on an isle within her family's grounds.
No soul her place can ever take,
Diana - Lady of the Lake!

Rena Soloman

Parting Song For Diana

Sweet angels carried thee to thy rest
And with music was borne into
Heaven's realm
Passing along a perfumed path of love
To stay within a scented bower
England's beloved loveliest flower
The moon to watch over you at night
The sun to shine on your beautiful place
At last away from prying sight
Those bowing trees protect your grace
We'll miss forever your radiant face
Our tears will be like the rain from above
Covering you gently with our cloak of love
Dearest Diana compassion's best
Sweet angels carried you to rest
You caused a nation's heart to beat as one
Laying wreathes and cards reluctant to leave

You who'd gone
You are not here
But haven't gone
Your love lives on.

Elizabeth Ruskin

Eternal Love

*In love divine for the world to see
Our Princes Diana meant so much
to you and to me.*

*God Almighty graced her
With a caring wonderful nature
Whose very Angel Personality
Gave love and hope to humanity.*

*Dear Diana, our Fairy-tale Royal Princess
In her great gift and role as a wife and a Mother
Showed in this greatest gift from God above
Mother love for Prince William and Prince Harry
Also in love for children everywhere
In them she will be loved and remembered Forever*

*Joy and Sadness tinged her life
Yet, she held her head up high
In dignity Brave Caring Diana reached her goal
Blessed by Mother Teresa
In her gift for help to the Rich, the Poor
and the Needy*

*A candle of love that will always be aflame
In her Epitaph wonderful Diana
is loved and remembered in Eternal
love for everyone*

. . .

Most of all she touched the lives of people all ages
Now our Princess is resting peacefully
In Jesus forever more
In her beloved island home carpeted in a million flowers
Where she is free and bluebirds sing
Such love shown by humanity to our
Princess of Hearts
And in Children everywhere praying and giving.

Maureen J Archibold

In Memory Of Princess Diana

The Princess of Wales and our nation's Rose,
Why you left us, nobody knows.
A light in our hearts, that has now burnt out,
We'll always remember you, without a doubt.

The Queen of Hearts, full of sunshine
and light,
You fought for the people, never gave up
without a fight,
You helped out the world, though it brought
you pain,
You gave so much, but had nothing to gain.

You disappeared like early morning dew,
This is for you Diana, we love you.

Kirsty Davies

Diana Princess Of Wales

*Pain, pain and more pain
can make one's life seem in vain
To overcome this hopeless task
Diana did more than was asked*

*To help the poor the old the sick
through her own experience of the rich
No-one will know the loneliness she endured
it now comes out, be assured*

*By helping others in their pain
gave her courage much more to gain
Inspired her life behind the beauty
the facade of abuse, supposed duty*

*She bucked the system in a way
giving pleasure, just to say
Help is there you're not alone
stricken faces with no home*

*True kindness of giving, no-one knowing
so many times, her only way of showing
A charmed life some might say
the pointing finger comes back your way*

*She never wore a judge's cap
any child lay on her lap
In God's eyes she did her best
now her soul is laid to rest*

*Kindness comes in many guises
in her heart she chose the wisest
Her epitaph can only be
in helping others sets you free . . .*

Jean Tennent Mitchell

A Queen Of Hearts

She was ours for just a little while
Our own Princess of Wales
Now sadly, we are mourning
In the Hills and in the Vales

Nations followed in her steps
To try to get wrongs righted
Our Ambassador of care and love
Wished the World to be united

She trod where others feared to tread
Despite any objection
Did a job that needed doing
And she did it . . . to perfection

A Joan of Arc of modern times
She battled on with zest
Fighting for the sick and needy
Complying with each quest

Her time with us was limited
Like a beautiful butterfly
She flew away and left us
Now we're left to wonder . . . Why?

We'll remember her as she would wish
Over the coming years
'A Queen of Hearts' without a Crown
Whilst the World wears a Coronet of Tears.

Bell Ferris

The Fairy-Tale Princess

Shy and vulnerable, she entered our hearts,
Marrying a man of great power.
Now, when we feel this sadness inside,
We recall that memorable hour.

She stole the hearts of everyone,
From the United Kingdom to Perth.
She was the Eighth Wonder of the World,
Loved by everyone on this earth.

She went beyond the line of duty,
To help anyone in need,
The sick she would look after,
The hungry she would feed.

Even in the times of pain,
She put on a smile.
Always in the 'Public Eye',
Always under trial.

The nicest person you could ever have met,
Tried to help everyone she saw,
But this caring nature that she had
The 'Press' saw as a flaw.

She had smiling, sparkling eyes,
Her face never showed a frown.
But the 'Press' did all they could
To put our Princess down.

They would never let her,
Live her life the way it should be.
They tried to control her all the time.
They would not let her be free.

Now, for this Fairy Tale Princess,
Our nations mourn together
For this wonderful woman,
Who will be remembered forever.

Her two sons are left behind
To face the struggles, the pain.
We pray for them, they're in our hearts,
As our tears fall like rain.

Our beautiful Princess Diana
Who will never be replaced,
Was taken from us, when for the first time it seemed,
With happiness she was graced.

So now our Fairytale Princess,
Is looking after us from above.
The mother, the helper, the carer, the sharer,
The peacemaker, the dove.

Rachael Taylor (15)

My Tribute For Princess Diana Is . . .

Deep is the loss we feel,
In our hearts you will always be.
All the world mourns you.
No-one will ever replace you,
Always to be remembered.

Rest in peace sweet Princess.
Goodnight and God bless.

Victoria Hogan

Diana's Lullaby

Once in every million years
the world is steeped in shame.
Its people cry a million tears
as love reveals its name

Once in every million years
a new bird sings its song
and though death deals its mighty blow
the melody lives on.

The melody is soft and sweet
to new-born babies' ears,
Diana's loving lullaby
to wash away the tears.

And time and tide mean nothing now
The strength is in the song.
Her lullaby of life and love
Forever marches on.

Margaret Wendt

Diana Princess Of Wales

Diana Princess of Wales
You will never be forgotten
You're one in a million we all love you
Those little children you went to see
Hold them in your loving arms for a cuddle

People with AIDS you held their hands
You gave them love and comforted them
You visited the homeless with your sons
People will miss you our loving Princess

In Paradise together you and Dodi
Praying now you'll both
Be able to Rest In Peace
You've left behind sweet memories

Lisa Wyatt

Eulogy To A Princess

Diana, our loving Princess of Wales,
Your memory will remain evermore,
In our hearts and minds it will never fail,
For you were a special person, to adore,
Time and again you will return, in all ways,
Your good works to prove you were here,
For so many, they brought better days,
As you dispelled their worries and fear.

Your achievements inspired us all,
For your dream of a fairer world,
Throughout our lives, your vision to recall;
We shall strive on, your flag unfurled,
Until the innocent shall survive,
And shall not needlessly be slain;
God's little children enabled to thrive,
Not allowed to endure endless pain.

We will never forget our angel of light,
Though you have gone so far away,
Your vision will shine thro' the darkest night,
And carry us forward, by your golden ray.

Julia Eva Yeardye

A Tribute To Princess Diana

You gave your all,
To the people.
Even when in distress
You found this gave you,
Strength to carry on -
To love others
To give them hope and joy
To help the sick and elderly
To get the Ban of Mines
Your inspiration to others,
Will be remembered -
The whole World over
A True Mother
The Queen of Hearts
Now in God's hands at Peace.

Gladys Davenport

Only A Minute

It's over; just like that - no more
My soul is raw
I can't believe
My eyes - my ears
This thing - this death that takes your life.
An end to strife -
No shining light
To warm our nights.
Your beauty echoes ever on
You will live on
In hearts of ours
For love goes far.

Elizabeth Mitchell

The Smile Of Love

A shy young girl worked at a nursery
  Loving children, all of her life,
She met, and was courted by a Prince
  Who then made her his wife.

It was a fairytale wedding
  A beautiful bride on that July day.
With plenty of laughing and cheering
  And a kiss, on the balcony - so gay.

A son was born soon after
  Who would eventually be Heir to the Throne.
Two years later, he had a brother,
  So now, he was no longer alone.

Their mother loved them deeply
  She shared their sorrows and joys.
Love and happiness radiated from her,
  When she was with her two boys.

Divorce and unhappiness followed,
  Her life went a different way.
Her love for the young, the aged, the sick,
  Was seen in her caring, each day.

Her life was to end so sudden,
  Her love, still never fails.
To touch the hearts of the people,
  Diana, Princess of Wales.

Joan Smith

Diana Princess Of Love Remembered

D iana
I can
A nd will
N ame you
A gain

      P rincess
      R ighteousness,
      I will sing your
      N ame,
      C herish your
      E ntity, to
      S weep away
      S orrow.

O bituary;
F orever

      L over
      O f the
      V ictims of
      E arth.

R emembered,
E very time
M an is unjust.
E very time
M an is intrusive,
B eckoned by greed.
E very time
R eason is lacking.
E very time
D eath is sudden!

Linda Coleman

Chronicle Of Memories

Your name incites fond memories
a teenager so innocent and shy,
a fairytale wedding,
a spectacular dress,
veiled, was your beautiful smile.

Adoringly we watched you grow,
such startling beauty and grace,
your elegance was unsurpassed
and your vibrancy as a mother admired.

You camouflaged your sadness well,
we knew nothing of your pain,
then we learned of your own self-doubts,
your secret ills and loss in love,
It broke all our hearts that we could not help.

Dying children cradled in your arms,
your hands touched a man with AIDS,
your compassion truly knew no bounds,
you addressed our ignorance and fears,
we the guilty, hung our heads in shame.

You are dead.

Stunned silence befalls us all,
a nation and a world are in mourning,
seas of flowers and oceans of tears
for a cherished princess,
but forever now a Queen in Heaven.

Jacki McEneaney

Simply Diana

*Diana was an English Rose,
A rose beyond compare,
With beautiful complexion,
And hair so very fair.*

*She really was a Princess,
Spreading joy wher'er she went,
Reaching out to those in need,
No barriers would she heed.*

*Then there was the pleasantest job,
The one she loved the best,
The one she did most willingly,
Of being a loving Mum.*

*Her own life sometimes wasn't fun,
But she came smiling through,
And brought to people's notice,
Things that they would rather shun.*

*Now she's no longer with us,
And we all feel in despair,
Especially her family,
Who loved her more than all.*

*But her memory will linger on,
Of the causes she has fought,
Of her comfort, care and laughter,
And her legacy of love.*

Matthew J Prescott (12)

Diana

All your people wept for you.
They cheered for you, to show they care.
They prayed and sang for you,
To show you on your way,
To meet and guide
The angels in heaven

You will be greatly missed
By the poor, the maimed and ill,
You touched us all.
With your strength to fight,
People will carry on
Your good work for the needy,
Knowing you are watching,
Making sure your work
Continues the way you would want.

Don Jeffery

A Star Shines Brightly

Diana, Princess of Wales,
fair lady of children's fairy tales
though no longer with us in the flesh
you still live on in hearts and minds afresh.
And when I look out at the stars tonight
and see one twinkling,
bigger and brighter than the rest.
I call it the Diana star,
reflecting your image from afar
and that is the one, I love the best

Doris Dobbins

Our Princess

You were a bud
That opened in bloom
You married a prince
Yet your dream was shattered
But we all loved you Diana
That's what mattered
But now our flower has gone
But to the world you were the one
Whom we loved and adored
How we will miss you
That beautiful flower
That died
Now you have gone
How all the world cried
You will be sadly missed
We send you our love
Sealed with a kiss.

P M Wardle

On Your Island Of Dreams

A scented rose, the striking lily,
Blue delphinium eyes in enhanced repose.
Lie within a magnificent sentinel array of flowers
Upon your Island of Dreams.

Do not be afraid, the Royal Court protagonists
And one-eyed pack should be pitied and forgiven.
The People's Coronation of Wreaths
Will not wither, in time they will gently blossom.

Do not weep sweet young princes,
Mummy would not want to see you cry.
She is with you, just listen inside.
Diana is within all her people.

Jackie Goldsworthy

Diana

Sleep well, sweet gentle Princess,
You've more than proved your worth;
Not just to God in Heaven,
But to all of us on Earth.
Your loving glance and tender touch,
No matter where you went,
Plainly showed to all the World,
That you were Heaven-sent.
So rest in peace, sweet Princess,
Now God has called you home;
No-one could e'er forget you,
Nor all the love you've shown.
As you, sweet gentle Princess,
Upon your island lie,
Like petals, we will blanket you,
With love that cannot die.
You shared with us your everything,
Your blessings, sorrows, joys,
Leaving us the legacy,
Of your two precious boys.
Sleep well, sleep well, Diana,
Our brightest shining star,
You made our World a better place,
Yet shimmer still afar.

Betty Taylor

Many Years Of Love

Many years of love, of anger and of pain,
Many years of sorrow, of hope and of blame.
Many years of pictures, we felt we knew you well,
Many years of being betrayed, of 'kiss 'n' tell'.

Many years of caring, the joy that you brought,
Many years of sheer hard work, the battles
                              that were fought.
Many years of comfort for the old and the meek,
Many years of giving love to the young and
                                      the weak.

Many years of friendship for ones you
                              hardly knew,
Many years of grace and beauty that were
                              unique to you.
Many years of pride for your precious ones,
Many years of laughter with your growing sons.

Now not so many years you had,
Too far and few between,
But in our hearts for many years,
You'll always be our Queen.

Susan W Robinson

Diana - (Voice Of The World)

Such a need for life -
Such a loss in death -
The world lost its voice -
When she lost her breath.

W G Royce

Rose In Paris

A Rose was crushed in Paris
Taken when blooming in kindness, love
                                  and maturity,
Victim of circumstance, machine and mankind
And now blame is sought,
Is it this, is it that, is it him?
All are hounded in the hunt for retribution,
They all must pay.

God wanted this Rose in his garden
He took perfection and replanted it on high,
A blameless Rose was needed, an example
                                  to us all,
The Rose will bloom forever
It would not have wanted 'blame',
Let the Rose rest in peace and tranquillity
Let love and forgiveness reign.

Gillian Ackers

Diana Sweet Princess

How many tears must we shed to bring you back?
Oh why did you have to leave us, when you
touched our hearts in a special way?
We will never forget your warm loving caring,
and the smile and joy you brought to
people's lives.
        Rest in peace Sweet Angel.

Darren Hennessy & Family

September Sadness

When the world stood still
  and the stars went dim
The leaves on the trees
  hung silent and still
Something happened to the world
  like a knife in the heart
Such pain - such sadness
  no words can impart
It's not fair to take her
  she had love to share
It's not fair - we need her
  to show us she cared.
Life can be ugly and so unfair
Was she too beautiful for us mortals?
Did heaven need her - too much to share?

G Tominey

A Tribute To Diana
(The nation's Queen of Hearts)

Your kindness was a loving word
Your kindness was a helping hand
Loving persons beneath her rank
Performing so many difficult tasks
Visiting the sick, young and old
She succeeded with flying colours,
To me she was not only the Queen of Hearts
But a saint in disguise
May she rest in peace
        Never to be forgotten.

Gilbert Harford

A Tribute To Diana Princess Of Wales

*A beautiful fairytale princess
From a fairytale country,
You were a dream come true,
An inspiration to its people;
Now a loss to the world
The saintly Queen of Hearts
You sure moved mine
You touched my hand, you smiled serene.
Now an angel in the sky
Smile down on me
And fill me anew, I miss you so much,
I cherish your memory
And I always will.
God bless you.*

Catherine Mary Smerdon

Diana

D iana you were the finest jewel in England's
   golden crown.
I n your short life Princess of the
   People you shone.
A lways ready to show the world
   you cared.
N ow and forever your goodness and
   beauty will still live on.
A s heaven claims back its brightest
   star to wear.

Pauline Christina Knight

Sleep Now, Sleep
(Dedicated to the memory of Diana -
The Princess of Wales)

When the famous die one feels sadness
Yet this is different.
A figure of debate, controversy, pity.
She touched our lives
She touched the world.
Why does such beauty and love leave us now?
Maybe this earth did not deserve her
Maybe Deity requires her.
A fairy-tale Princess who cared, who noticed.
Supporting foundations donating her time,
Such time which now seems precious.
Her beacon of light shines forever.
An indelible mark left behind,
Not surpassed for centuries.
The world was your family you nurtured
and hugged,
For decades will pass when we'll crave for
your goodness.
But the angels will sing to their wondrous arrival
They'll value this asset not drag through
the gutter.
Sleep now, sleep.
The pain is over, the parasites have gone.
Your prophecy foretold a legend now born.
A figurehead of souls
The real 'Queen of Hearts'.

Nicholas William James

A Sea Of Tears Out Of Sadness

Today there is a sea of tears around the world
Tears from the inner soul, are like open prayers
Each tear, has a thought of compassion, of love,
a feeling of losing a friend, whose young life came
to an end.

Today God has sent a sea of flowers from each
and every heart, an aroma of love fills the air.
The velvet petals, alikened to the GRACE which
Diana shared, soft and gentle to those for whom she cared.

Today the world stood still to share peace and
sadness, of at times an unseen angel behind
the scenes.
To the poor, afflicted, tiny children, she was
a Queen.
Today the atmosphere was of God, all around,
the hurting he upheld, the unbelieving believed.
Today we came together to mourn a Mum, who
loved and adored her sons.
Today the sons followed their Queen, who gave
them love and hugs and life's perspective.

Today the air stood still, the coming of change in
the human heart, the remaking of history the
new young King, the common part, the scenes of
which young and old will never see again.

Days ago Diana's soul had returned to her
Heavenly Home but her gentle spirit is in the air.
Loved, not forgotten, her seeds and fruits shall
live on forever in the nation's heart.

B Fletcher

Lady Of The Lake

You are our Lady of the Lake,
Lying on your lonely island,
With the flowers all around.
Lady of the Lake.
And the lilies and the roses and the sweet,
                                      sweet wind
That blows the smoke of candles in my eyes.
And the anger and the anguish and the deep,
                                      deep grief
As the nation cries.

He's just a beggar in the street,
Lying in his lonely doorway,
With the rubbish all around.
Beggar in the street.
And the litter and the dustbins and the sour,
                                      sour wind
That blows the dust of London in his eyes.
Oh the anger and the anguish and the deep,
                                      deep grief
As a beggar cries.

She went to him and held his hand
Gave him hope and found him shelter
Thawed the ice inside his heart.
She held his hand.
And now he brings the lilies to her palace gates
And wipes the tears of sadness from his eyes
As the sea of flowers rises from the deep,
                                      deep grief
As a nation cries.

For the lovely Lady Di.

Janna Eliot

A Picture Of Tragedy

Diana, Princess of Wales
Our Queen that never was
The prima donna of our country
With eyes of adoration
Revealing your love for Dodi
Your dignity, warmth and caring
Was the realism of life
You touched the hearts of all nations
As no one had done before you
You invigorate the sick, and wounded
The ones others redeemed untouchable
In life, you were a saint
In an evil, corrupt, and greedy world
We will mourn your loss, Diana
And forever, have tear-stained cheeks
As our ruby red eyes still weep for you
Your diamond sparkling eyes, and smile
Have gone from reality
Prevail on Diana
In the hearts of all nations
We beg of you
Live on in heaven
For the love of Dodi
You will live on in death
Deep within our hearts,
Forever more.

RIP Diana, and Dodi.

Sylvia M Coulson

BBC1 London, September 6th 1997

Today, we in our millions, saw
The scarlet tunics and the gold
Which found no place in her.
We saw the million sombre faces
Of the shocked and silent crowd
Who had come unbidden
To mourn her loss
As the cortege cast long shadows
In the low September sun.

We heard the minutes counted
By one lonely tolling bell,
The slow clop of unhurried hooves
Which gave us time to ponder
As she passed:
The jingle of the harness,
At times, the sound of muffled weeping.
The grind of heavy wheels
Across Horse Guards Parade.

And, amidst it all,
High above the trappings,
The jewel, which was Diana,
Glowed in the autumn light,
Wrapped in the Royal Standard,
Crowned by the waxen white
Of her loved ones' flowers,
As we said goodbye
To the funny, fragile, loving girl -
The queen who never was
Save, as she wished to be
In our hearts, this day
And in a special way,
For ever.

John Matthews

Litany Of Diana

We will remember your courage
We will remember your caring
And compassion in all its strength
We will remember you Diana
      Princess of Wales
      Queen of Hearts
      Rose of England
      Help of the Needy
      Comforter of the Sick
      Refuge of the Homeless
      Lover of Children
      Friend of the World.

WHAT MAN COULD HAVE DONE MORE

Mary Seddon

Beloved Diana

In memoriam, in sympathy
Beloved Diana
Princess of hearts

Diana
Pure in soul
Pure in heart
tainted by life
touched with love

'twas divine intervention
dark forces to part
hosts of angels
save a light of the world so bright
light shines forth - triumphant
to herald thy way
be guided and let thy spirit rise

In your life's path and people's
there is a lesson for all
some may rise now but some may still fall
mirrors of love, mirrors of lust
mirrors of sorrow, now mirrors of dust

Who are we?
We the hypocrites who dare to point and judge
judge oneself
then be silent

In loving memory
We search our souls.

Lynne Stuart

The Silent Scents Of Remembrance
*(Written after a visit to the Palaces of Kensington
and Buckingham and St James and to Harrods, 3.9.97)*

I will always remember
The sombre silence
The incredible quiet
Enveloping such crowds of ordinary people
The silent vigil and gentle tears of everyone
                                      around me
The sharing of sorrow in whispers with
                              complete strangers
The very serene homage that I felt so privileged
To be part of.
I will always remember
The scented air
Perfumed with musk and frankincense and myrrh
from so many candles
The deep and unforgettable scent of so many
                                        white lilies
The sweet aroma from such a sea of flowers
Pervading the Park and Palaces and along
The Mall and in front of Harrods
Drifting from the trees and the railings and from
the ground and the pavements
Into the hearts of her people and beyond.

I will always remember.

Barbara Keeling

Funeral Of Diana, Princess Of Wales
(Written while watching the television broadcast)

Silence, oh the enveloping silence
So overwhelming. So emotional.

Only the horses' hooves
Clicking of brass against leather
Soldiers precise marching shoes on tarmac
and the every minute muffled bell
accompanied a gun-carriage coffin
on a bright sunlit unique occasion.

White tulips and lilies
Placed on top of the Royal Coat of Arms
never realised how the World
would focus on their simplicity.

How many tears fell from public and private eyes
during that monumental procession
through London streets,
that showed unimaginable respect towards
                                      an individual
who also showed great respect
and interest
and compassion and love
to those of lesser upbringing?

A sadder moment in history never existed . . .?

John Ernest Day

Diana
Princess - Super Star

Born infinitely blessed, she wore an easy grace
that lingered in the mind,
the kind of form and face possessed
by rarest chance, to last a lifetime's span:

a single glance could fell the strongest man,
with women too, held captive by her eyes.

There seemed no limit to such charm as hers,
A God-grown gift, designed to scorn the spite
of passing years:
like peerless crystal, shining and unflawed,
she drew whatever light was there to find,
and adulation grew.

Then, somewhere in the shadows,
                    mischief stirred,
cruel rumours gathered pace and
                    spread distrust,
with brutal thrust of words combined to shame
the blameless life, by fortune made so sweet.

Sorely, she felt sharp chill of malice in the air,
yet, with disarming flair,
as swiftly charmed away the hate,
to halt wild spate of gossip in its run,
for no barbed, vengeful story, could denigrate
                                to dust,
the glory and acclaim - so fairly won.

June White

The Blossoming Of Diana The White Rose

*Diana you came into our lives
as a shy violet hiding your beauty amongst
the leaves. We knew you were there your
perfume filled the air around us.*

*Like a snowdrop you bowed your head
but your pure beauty still shone through.*

*Your sparkling eyes as blue as the
forget-me-not shone with compassion.*

*Your tall slim figure like the lily
which you loved.*

*As fragrant as the exotic orchid
you wore in your hair.*

You were always there.

*As the English Rose your beauty grew.
Rising above the cruel thorns
to emerge into the sunlight.*

*So will you always be remembered
as we covered you with flowers
to rest in peace in the garden
of your home.*

*Safe in the Arms of God.
And always in our hearts.
   Rest in Peace. English Rose.*

Pauline Morris

Memories Of A Beautiful Princess

As beautiful and graceful as a swan,
She brought happiness into this world.
Now she has sadly departed,
From this world, to a beautiful paradise.

Memories of her good deeds are in our minds,
Her warm and tender ways.
To find another woman like her is impossible,
She was so beautiful and unique.

The whole world mourns for our lovely princess,
How quickly she left us in torment.
Our world will never be the same,
But she will be remembered eternally.

She brought smiles to even the saddest of faces,
The warmth in her heart could have lit
*   a thousand fires.*
And like her kindness stay alight forever,
Warming up the entire world with her love.

She was never selfish, everyone else was put
*   before herself,*
She was such a generous, thoughtful person.
In our hearts she will remain forever,
Alive and full of passion.

She shone with beauty and radiance,
We all loved and admired her.
But we never did show her how much we cared,
And now it is too late.
*   Memories of a beautiful princess.*

Lisa Frost (14)

Rest A While

*Rest a while
On the lull of the evening,
Let the ebb tide of the day
Wash away any sadness.
Let the memories
of the day's goodness
resonate within you
As you drift towards
The dimming of your day.
For if you hold in your heart
A cherished memory,
What more could you have asked for?
Rest a while
On the lull of the evening,
Let the ebb tide of the day
Wash away any regrets.
Let the memories
Of the love you feel
Envelop you
As it eases your passage
Into the embrace of your night.
For if you have loved
And been so loved,
What more could you have hoped for?
So rest a while
On the lull of the evening,
Let your goodness
Let your love
Return on the tide
Of someone else's day.*

Jacqueline Gilbert

Diana

Diana,
Bright Star of our firmament.
So cruelly torn away from out our midst,
By those whose sole desire was gain,
For a photograph or two.
So great your fame,
Throughout this globe, that we call Earth.

Beauty, compassion, kindness,
And the common touch,
Were those reflections of your soul;
That meant so much,
To all who met you on life's way.
Great or small, disabled, maimed
Or sick. Homeless, bereaved or just simply lost.
You gathered them within your love;
Gave them comfort rare.
And did not stop to count the cost.

Now, in ever-flowing stream they come,
Their grateful thanks to say,
With flowers, a word or more,
And patiently wait for many hours,
In winding queues, outside the doors.
To enter on each open page,
Their own small tributes,
To a miracle of our age.
In their own words.
Diana, queen of our hearts.
God in His mercy grant you peace.

Stella J Jefferies

To Diana

Today I went to sign the condolence book for you
 in the Town Hall in Leigh,
I couldn't believe the queues there were, waiting
 so very patiently.
No-one grumbling, no pushing, no jostling, to get
 to the front of the queue,
All, everyone wanted was a chance to write down
 their thoughts on you.
You were lovely and admired so much by people
 young and old everywhere,
Because you weren't afraid to step into the
 unknown and you were a princess who really
 did care.
We'll miss you more than words can ever say,
But for some reason God decided to take
 you away.

D Ridings

Diana Princess Of Wales

D is for Devotion and affection
I   is for Inner love and kindness
A is for Assurance and confidence you gave
N is for Nobody was too high or low to whom
         you gave your love too
A is for All the people who you brought love and
         kindness to in your life.
                  Our Diana

Ronald Finnighan

In Memory Of Diana, Princess Of Wales

She walked in beauty,
Bright as any star,
Touching the world, with love,
As she passed by,
This 'Queen of Hearts', God lent us,
For a while,
To warm and brighten,
Earth's dark corners,
With her smile,
But though no more, her happy face,
We'll see,
Through death, she'll reign,
Queen of all hearts, forever,
In our memory.

Barbara I Grove

Farewell To Diana

I saw the clouds scurrying along the sky
to say a last farewell to Diana.
The sunlight shimmered on the lake
breaking into a thousand fragments
like the hearts that break for Diana.
A white rose sheds dewdrop tears for Diana.
Stars shone brightly in the depth of night,
to pay homage to Diana, and yet
though we lived through the darkest of nights
then came the dawn and the breeze with the
dawn whispered rest in peace, all is well with
                                        Diana.

Lindy Ess

Diana

A nation of tears, how one person in death can
give so much grief to so many people, the castle
ruins of life then the searching, to rebuild the
outer walls.

The sweet smell of the rain bringing new love to the flowers of life,
tree branches opening up their hearts, calling in all nature's love.

Fighting out of the thickets, the country lane at
peace and love, no one in life should be empty of love, such a small
word that can put into life what no other word can.

If there is someone in life that can hold you, look into your eyes,
romance you with the power of love, taking you on a journey of
passion, trust lighting candles in your life, never to be blown out.

The calling of time we can't understand, the towers of the castle
rebuilt, a new love of life starting, why the angry clouds, drizzling
rain, the flagpole broken apart, the new flag of life wet and
drooping, this love should never a dreadful word, died.

Garrett John

Happiness

Happiness is yellow
It tastes like melting toffee
It smells like cut grass
It is a bowl of juicy fruit
It sounds like birds tweeting,
and thinking of the beautiful
      Princess Diana.

Mark McFall (10)

To Diana

How dark this night,
Even the stars are weeping.
The moon, aware of earth's great tragedy
Hides, silent,
In deference to that brighter light
That only yesterday illumed the world.
How short a time since darkness came.
Impossible to think it was but yesterday,
It seems, in grief and tears, to be a lifetime.
Oh how earth grieves.
Flowers and candles like a girdle round the earth
Speak of love.
Were ever hearts and minds so stunned,
Blood so chilled as on this day.
As one the nation mourns.
The bonds of grief unite like bands of steel.
Heart against heart folk stand
United in pain and a million different memories.
Surely love like this will soar to Heaven's gates.
Rest well sweet Diana, assured that in death
As in life, every heart is yours
And ever will be.

Peggy Adams

Lady Di

*You came into our lives a Princess
You leave with shock and wonder.
We thought you had finally found
happiness in Dodi.
But your happiness was short-lived.*

*At least you were with the one you loved
when tragedy struck.
We all hope and pray that you are with him now
and for evermore.
The only sadness is for your two sons who are left
behind to cope with the loss of their beloved
mother and friend.*

*Our thoughts and prayers are with them both
you gave so much to so many people
those who were lucky enough to meet you can
only begin to feel the loss that William and Harry
feel.*

*You were an inspiration to many and you will
never be forgotten
You always put people especially the old, the
young and the sick first -
Even though you suffered so much unhappiness
you were always there for other people.*

*I never had the chance to meet you but I feel that
I know you.
But I still feel very unhappy about the very tragic
way you had to die.*

They always say the good die young . . .
God knows he has got one of the best in you
I hope and pray that wherever you are, you are with those you loved who have left this world and entered the next.

I hope that Princes William and Harry can learn to accept your death given time.
Taking a little comfort in the fact that you were happy.
That you had finally found some happiness with Dodi.

At least now you are out of the way of the photographers forever, you can be what you want when you want.
The ones who followed you should be made to pay but they won't be!
They deserve the strongest punishment available but if you were here you would probably forgive them as you were that kind of person.

You will be dearly missed by everyone
Our beloved Lady Di.

Lisa Hobden

She Deserved Respect And She Got It

A quiet calm, invaded me
the depth, to yet, I have never felt
twas here, so deep inside my soul
that throbbed, pulsated, in agony
twas a hurt so fierce that none could help
except for to sit in its mournful presence
to ponder, to wonder, to try to absorb
and to question the reasons why?

And there we stood in silent reverence
we mourned as one, a throbbing unity
a chain of emotions reaching throughout
                                        the land
an agony of shock that ran from nation to nation
a silence that stemmed from the roots of despair
a silence that hung like a man from the gallows
a silence that said more than words ever would
a silence that only pain could effect

As our eyes fiercely followed her casket of abode
we allowed us to dwell on the memory of her
and the meaning of life, of her sadness
                                        and hopes
of her insecure feelings yet her abundance of love
of her desire for life, and her spirit of freedom
of her tortured and passionate love for her boys

This then we turned and watched them walk
down the path of dignified heartache
so slow, as grief marked their every step
so weary, as pain sat on burdened shoulders
so bitter, at the loss of one so rare
so sad as their grief spanned the ocean wide
yet astounded by the love, her people showed
and proud to know she was really Queen

Esther Austin

Diana

One true English rose
pure in heart and mind
born with no thorns
only goodness and kindness that shone from
             within
loved by oh so many people
born to be our Queen
yet was not to be
but you gave us two heirs
and your kindness will live on
from the love you have given them
and in every heart around the world
our Queen of Hearts you have become
the flowers placed in London Town
and all around the world when you died
showed that you were loved by everyone
So Diana, Queen of our Hearts
rest in peace now on your island in the lake.

Pauline Haggett

Silence

Silence!
Only the birds singing lovely humming sounds,
No sound of cars in the air,
People moving quietly,
Noses sniffing,
Sniff, sniff
Scent of flowers,
Fills the air.
Silence!
Only the people talking,
In hushed whispers all around,
People weeping,
Feet moving,
Slow and steady down The Mall.
Silence!
Bouquet upon bouquet,
A million bunches lay on the ground.
The wind flutters amongst the cards,
With one thought,
They all say,
We really miss you,
Diana, Princess of Wales.
Silence!

Jennifer Packham (9)

Diana

Slowly you entered our hearts
filling them with love
Treading where no woman
before you had dared
Reaching out to embrace
the world's untouchables,
the forgotten, the sick,
and giving so much to so many
until there was no more to give
An empty shell
wasted by man's heartless greed
Yet still you filled
a gaping wound with yours
'Midst mountains of fragrant petals
The nation's hearts beating as one.

Kay Rainsley

Untitled

There is a feeling of emptiness inside,
a sadness that wraps itself around us,
in our moments of silence.
We dare not think,
for to think brings tears.
We must remember the smile,
the beautiful eyes,
the kind heart.

Richard Irvine

Princess Of Smiles

A light was snuffed out in the world tonight,
A brightness extinguished for ever.
A warmth has been snatched so cruelly away.
Chilling all like a glacial river.

Her beauty and brightness shone out to all,
Like a beacon glows in the dark,
Her caring and kindness her love for all men,
Radiated straight from her heart.

So young and so vibrant; so full of life,
A beautiful person inside,
Then - gone in an instant of madness we're left
With our memories which never will fade.

To the world, a Lady of Royal Line,
A Duchess, a Princess of Wales,
For us on the street forever she'll be,
Diana, Princess of Smiles.

Margaret J H Goudie

Without You
(This poem has been created for Princess Diana)

Tomorrow will come without you,
How can I face it,
The people you helped,
The people you loved.

You had more love then anyone,
You had love to give,
You got people through their hard times,
You put everyone before yourself.

You touched so many hearts,
You never gave in,
The next day won't be the same,
I wish you didn't have to go.

Please Lord keep our Princess safe,
Please give her all the love you can give,
We will miss her every day within.

Kate Susan Douglas (15)

The Melody Lingers

Vulnerable and young
Her melody will continue
to be sung

She touched hearts
From every race and age

Wherever she went
With her support, charm and encouragement

A devoted mother
Though a troubled wife
With the help of therapies
Battled through to succeed

And as we look up to the skies
To mourn and pray
We must confess . . .
Too late
We valued in her brief life
Our compassionate
Princess!

Tamar Segal

Sombre Days

September morn,
sun arising changing our lives
leaving us in mourning.
A gift from heaven you cupped our hearts,
but now . . .
You depart.
Can we ever again, be the same?
Full of hope,
full of love for one so special.
Our doubts,
our fears are trebled without guidance to
light the world's path healing.
Our Diana.
Divine Invincible Angel of Nation. Amen . .

T A Peachey

Lament

Farewell Diana beloved.
Sharp fragments of past joys
Pierced our hearts, when your night fell
Upon the disbelieving world.
There can be no response
To mournful yearning,
Eternity has wrapped His
Heavenly mantle about you,
Protecting, loving, forgiving.
Sweet rest dear Princess.
Your earthly journey brief,
Will never be forgotten.

Cynthia Beaumont

Tribute To Diana

I am not ready yet for the sun to shine
or to join with the laughter of others
I am not ready
yet to smile beyond polite
or to hold any sense of meaning to life
I am not ready
yet to notice any sparkle of nature's glory
a sunrise or darkness are the same
Life continues because I breathe
I have no will nor reason
I am not ready
yet to fully live without her in this world
She whom this nation loves
and I who love her too.

B S Hansen

Tribute To Diana

One tear fell from heaven.
And the whole earth cried.
Stunned into silence
So young so beautiful
'Dear Diana,'
Touching hearts by mere chance.
Those shy eyes, my princess
Given to work, and so did.
With time for all
Dear, Dear, Diana.

Mick Philpot

Nos Star

The thunder roared,
The lightning flashed,
The mountains called out!
There's something wrong.
Then, the bad news -
'Yes, she has gone,'
The Lady of our land . . .
The choir in the valley stopped singing . . .
The Welsh were weeping because,
The Lady of our land has gone . . .
Bless you, Lady of the land . . .
But, Diana, we will never forget you . . .
So, we will lay the flag of our land
to the steps of heaven for you,
The Lady of our land . . .
The Welsh all love you, because you are
Diana, our Princess,
Always in our hearts . . .
We will carry your memory with pride and joy,
FOREVER,
You will always be,
The Lady of our land . . .

Richard Beck (14)

Princess Diana

*Diana you were the people's princess
Oh how we loved you so
Both the old and young alike
When you married Charles it was like a fairy tale
And unto you two sons were born
Who are now without a mum
You had many difficult and troubled times
In your short-lived life
But you were a very lovely person
Always reaching out to others
In their time of need*

*Young children you adored
And they loved you back
Your work was all worthwhile
You were making changes for the good
Then just as you had found love
And happiness in your life once again
God saw fit to take you away
The world will surely grieve for you
You will never be forgotten dear Diana
Your memory will always stay.*

Pamela Jewell

An Epitaph To A Real Lady

You were the one; the only one
We loved and adored, our
Treasured icon, so courageous;
Defying all adversities in a glance.

Beautiful; compulsive and ever watchful
You used your situation
For the wealth of millions,
For what does it take to give a smile
Or love to any man or woman, form or creed?

Our beloved Lady, you are
Gone now to a better place
And lay in grace and peace
Away from the ever-present and
Perverse evils of a sometimes too fast and
Modern world, that understood you
So well, yet never quite left you alone?
Goodbye our Lady, and may your spirit carry
Onward through time,
In our hearts, forever
As a lesson in love epitomised.
Goodbye.

Sue Jackett

Earth's Rainbow Of Love

Like a torch across the sky
Shooting stars added to dreams untold
Thunder and lightning gave warnings
A Rainbow circled the earth

Like an angel with wings outstretched
Clouds rolled by echoes of love moving
    Like magic all around

Heartbeats brought tears
People's thoughts stood still
Flowers forever blooming
The world dreams for-ever-as with love

Voices with feelings will ring
Bells will chime, memories will
    always be there
Life as with love brought happiness
Passing - brought sorrow

The green grass and hills with
    Flowers ever blooming
A loss never to be forgotten.

J S Mitchell

Dreams Of Light

You were the light in someone's shadow
offering laughter
Just one smile from you and they had
the light that you offered them.
Even though you have left
Your spirit lives on as each day passes.
If you look at the sky, we can see
the light that you gave others, carries on.
You were such a wonderful person
that God decided you had finished your duty
You have your freedom at last,
free as a bird.
Beautiful as a swan.

Mel Leggett

Queen Of Hearts

Rough autumn came too soon and seized
The rose of summer
Before her petals were unfurled
In mellowed splendour,
A rose encapsuled in our hearts
Forever vibrant,
The Queen of Hearts of all the world!

Denise Margaret Hargrave

Diana The World's Princess

You were the jewel in the crown.
And there was no one who could compare
With such a loving person as you.
Even though you have gone
On this sad August day
You will never be forgotten.
In our hearts you will always shine
Above anyone else.
When the world needed you
You came and helped
With your loving arms and words of kindness
Right from the beginning you chose your
                              path to follow.
So beautiful you were,
With a great shyness. But you were loved
In every corner of the world.
But you were sadly taken.
In your young life
You will always be remembered by all
That you will always be the jewel
Whose gem sparkled in the crown.

Ann Best

A Tribute

*Goodbye to our lovely Diana
Our own Princess of Wales
Who had been so kind-hearted
After all those damning tales*

*You lived your life for your two boys
As any mum would do
Which makes us want to hold on
To the memory of you*

*Sadly, we miss you
Since that fateful day
You answered the ultimate call
And tragically went away*

*Now that you're gone
Like a bird on the wing
Your never- fading love
Will guide us on the way*

*Your legend will live forever
For your humanity and will to win
As people to you were people
Not just anything*

Samantha

INFORMATION

We hope you have enjoyed reading this book - and that you will continue to enjoy it in the coming years.

If you like reading and writing poetry drop us a line, or give us a call, and we'll send you a free information pack.

Write to :-
**Poetry Now Information
1-2 Wainman Road
Woodston
Peterborough
PE2 7BU
(01733) 230746**